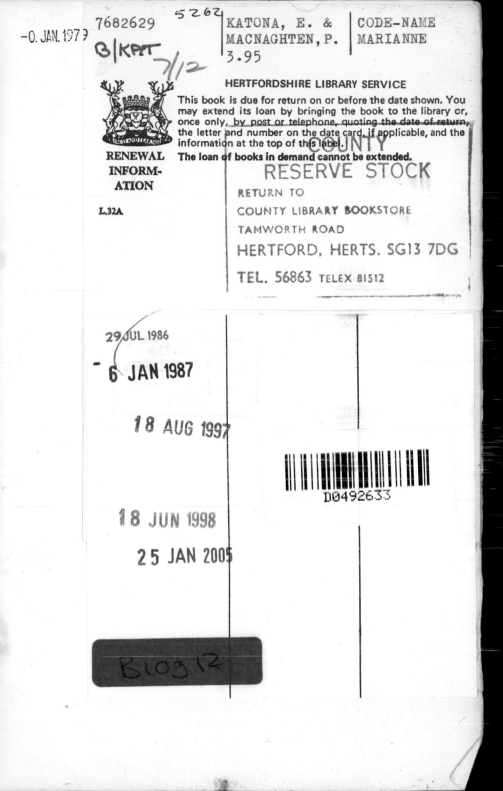

Code-Name Marianne

Code-Name Marianne

An Autobiography

Edita Katona with Patrick Macnaghten

Collins & Harvill Press
London 1976

© 1976 Edita Katona and Patrick Macnaghten
ISBN 0 00 262112 6
Set in Linotype Baskerville
Made and printed in Great Britain by
William Collins Sons & Co Ltd Glasgow
for Collins, St James's Place and
Harvill Press Ltd, 30A Pavilion Road
London SW1

To the memory of my mother

Illustrations

Contents of the Appendices
starting on page 211

Chapter 1

October 1938

'Can't I be a spy too?'

Colonel Petera looked at me in astonishment. Then suddenly he brought down his hand on the table with a thump, making the coffee cups rattle.

'That's my old friend's daughter!' he exclaimed, his eyes shining with pride. He had known me for all the twenty-four years of my life and now that Czechoslovakia had been occupied by the Nazis he, like my mother and myself, was an exile in Monte Carlo. For Mother, who spoke no French, he was the only person she could talk to and for me he was a link with the old happy life in Vienna. Although my father, like Eman Petera, had the Slav's intense love of his own country his business made it necessary for him to live in Vienna and it was there I had been brought up.

I loved my father deeply but on the day the Nazis marched into Vienna I was glad that he was dead. He would have felt, as I did, that the shame and the horror were almost unbearable. On 13 March 1938 Mother and I watched from the balcony of our flat as the Nazis goose-stepped down the broad street. They had started marching on the 11th but the official Occupation was on the 13th when the Chancellor, Doctor Schuschnigg, said good-bye to us and the Nazi flags waved in Vienna. Everybody, it appeared, was happy. It did not seem like an Occupation. It seemed like a reception.

It was time for us to go. We sold the flat and all the antiques which my parents had collected and cherished with such care over the years.

In those uncertain times, with the threat of a European war growing ever more immediate, nobody was much interested in antiques and we got absurdly little for them. Not that it mattered

9

because the only money we were allowed to take out of Austria amounted, when changed into Italian currency, to three thousand lire. If we had not stitched our less bulky pieces of jewellery into the seams of our clothes we would very soon have been destitute. But the jewellery was not enough to keep us very long so it was imperative that I should get a job. No hope was left now of fulfilling my lifelong ambition of training to become an actress. I worked for a time in the Casino in Venice, then we had to move again. Czechoslovakia was defying the Nazis and the Italian police warned us that if there should be war between Czechoslovakia and Germany we, with our Czech passports, would be interned.

In the event, of course, there was no war. The Czech forces, highly trained, superbly equipped and imbued with a fierce patriotism, were poised to defend their homeland. But on 30 September 1938 their British and French Allies signed away their cause in Munich.

But by that time Mother and I had crossed the border to Monte Carlo and it was there we bumped into my father's great friend, Eman Petera.

Now, sitting on the terrace of the Café de Paris, he told me that he had enrolled in the Deuxième Bureau and would be returning to Czechoslovakia to gather information which might help the Allies. He had no doubt that war was imminent.

'The Deuxième Bureau is the French espionage department,' he explained.

'Can you get me into it?' I asked eagerly. I envied him. The romance, the glamour, the freedom to travel. And, above all, the chance to join in the struggle against Hitler and the evil which was spreading like slime across Europe.

'I can try. There's a man called Sonnenschein, who recruits for them. He approached me. I'll have a word with him about you. They're desperately short of agents.'

Eman Petera smiled at me.

'And now, it's time for you to go back to your office.'

It was not really an office. When we first arrived in Monte Carlo I was dismayed to discover that without a work permit I could not get a job and that there was no chance of being given such a permit. My mother and I shared a room at a hotel but we could not stay there all day and we used to spend hours in a café, just sitting and spinning out our cups of coffee as long as possible. One afternoon I was looking idly at the local paper when an advertisement caught my eyes. It was for a secretary – must speak both German and French fluently. I did. 'Elegant and sophisticated' were other requirements. I still had the lovely dresses which the couturiers of Vienna had made for me in happier times, so I decided to apply. After all, the advertiser *might* not enquire about my work permit.

I was determined to get the job. If I did not find a way of earning money soon we should starve. This job would be the answer. I *must* get it.

If I want something very badly there is a force in me – as if there were a second me, both of us desperately wanting whatever it is. Not praying for it, just wanting it. And absolutely confident that we will get it. If you want something you have to be absolutely confident. If you allow yourself to doubt for one single second your willpower falters. You are lost. You are not convincing any more, you do not find the right words.

The letter answering the advertisement must, I realized, display some of the qualifications demanded. It was not necessary to write in several languages. The bald statement would be enough. But 'elegant and sophisticated'? I decided to use my own style, a light touch but with an underlying seriousness.

'Dear Sir, whoever you are.

Please consider my letter carefully because I need a job so badly. I am from Vienna and at my birth my Fairy Godmother bestowed on me the gift of tongues. Perfect German, Italian and French. I beg one more gift from her – this job.'

I addressed it to the box number, kissed it good luck and sent it on its way.

A few days later my Fairy Godmother, disguised as the postman, came. I was to go for an interview to an apartment in the Boulevard des Moulins, a very smart part of Monte Carlo.

A maid in a white apron showed me into a sumptuous drawing room and murmuring something I did not catch, left me alone. I was still gazing round the rich furnishings when an elderly man in a blue dressing gown came in. I recognized him instantly.

I had seen him often in Vienna. He was a rather mysterious Russian and he owned the Casino there.

'Mademoiselle Zukermanova! What are *you* doing here?'

'Monsieur Zimdin! What are *you* doing here? *I* have come for the job,' I told him.

'Well of course it's yours. How much do you want me to pay you?'

'I leave that entirely to your generosity, Monsieur Zimdin.'

He suggested a figure which would cover our hotel bill and leave something over for food. Secretaries were not highly paid in those days and this salary was more than I had expected.

Any misgivings I had about the nature of the job proved groundless. I was a secretary and nothing more. Monsieur Zimdin spoke not a word of French and I had to translate everything into German for him. He was building a really splendid villa with a swimming pool and mooring for his yacht, and often I went with him to consult the builder or the architect. Sometimes I was sent with a message and on these occasions I would be driven by Monsieur Zimdin's chauffeur in the Mercedes.

It was the chauffeur who told me how Monsieur Zimdin had laid the foundation of his fortune. Various Russian aristocrats had, after the Revolution, entrusted their jewels to him. He was to smuggle them into France where the owners would collect them. Monsieur Zimdin carried out his part of the task successfully but the owners of the jewels were shot. If these aristocrats had ever managed to reach France they could have lived comfortably on the proceeds of the sale of the jewels. In the event, Monsieur Zimdin did.

At first he treated me reasonably enough but gradually his attitude changed. He gave up saying 'please' and 'thank you' and particularly after he had had a row with one of his two mistresses, he took pleasure in humiliating me. He would throw the letters on the floor at my feet and watch with enjoyment while I stooped to pick them up. No mention was made of a work permit. However, Monsieur Zimdin knew as well as I did that I did not have one and he had begun to take advantage of the fact.

But it was not only the prospect of getting away from Monsieur Zimdin and his dreary job which made me hug myself with excitement. Ever since I was a little girl I had longed to be an actress, to sweep across a stage with all eyes on me, to strike poses and postures, to be the centre of attention and admiration. I suppose that because I was an only child I tended more than most to live in a world of fantasy, to make up long stories which I would act out on my own, happy to be solitary.

And now here was the opportunity to act out a part more exciting, more glamorous, more romantic than any I could ever have created in my own imagination. And it would be real. Far, far better than any make-believe role. There would never be that awful anti-climax when the curtain comes down and you sit in your dressing room rubbing the greasepaint off your face. In real-life espionage the greasepaint must never come off.

That evening I kept very silent at first, not telling my mother anything about my talk with Petera for I did not want to raise false hopes in either of us – besides my hopes would have been her fears. But in the end I mentioned casually, playing it down, that Eman Petera might be able to get me a job with the Deuxième Bureau. I was deliberately vague about the function of the Bureau and Mother did not pursue the matter. She took it as I had hoped she would, as the possibility of a better job, without considering its implications. Even when, the next day, Eman Petera told her that he was returning to Czechoslovakia to spy for the French she was sad only because he was leaving Monte Carlo. It did not seem to occur to her that he might be going into danger.

'Sonnenschein has arranged an interview with these people for you,' Eman told me, 'on Thursday.'

'The day after tomorrow! That's quick.'

'These people work fast. You are to be in the Cristie Bar in Nice at three o'clock. Do you know it?'

'No, I've only been to Nice once. But I'll find it.'

'It's in the Boulevard Victor Hugo.'

Wednesday dragged and dragged. On Thursday morning I put on my prettiest dress and took special care with my hair and my make-up. Fortunately Monsieur Zimdin was lunching out so I was able to slip away without having to give an explanation.

During the forty-minute bus ride to Nice I had plenty of time to think about the forthcoming interview. It had been important

13

to me to be successful at the interview with Monsieur Zimdin but this was infinitely more important. The most important thing in my whole life. I just *had* to bring it off.

I had no idea what form the meeting might take. But I knew that there would be one crucial moment. My whole future would depend on how I behaved on the spur of that moment. It was as if I had been preparing for it ever since I was born. I was like an archer tautening his bow, pulling it back inch by inch until it would stretch no farther and the time had come to release the arrow on its flight to the target.

I had allowed plenty of time and it was not difficult to find the Boulevard Victor Hugo, one of the main thoroughfares of Nice. Consequently it was a few minutes before three o'clock when I descended the steps leading to the Cristie Bar. In the evening, when there was dancing, this elegant room would be crowded, but all along the Mediterranean three o'clock in the afternoon is the hour of the siesta and so I found it deserted except for two waiters standing by the long bar and three men at a table in the corner. One of them glanced up as I came in and then looked away again. A waiter came forward and drew out a chair for me at a table near the bar.

'I won't order anything yet, thank you,' I said. 'I'm waiting for some friends.' I had only just enough money for the bus fare back to Monte Carlo – none to spare for coffee.

There was a big round clock on the wall opposite me and I watched as it approached three o'clock. Then two minutes past three, five minutes past three, ten. Nobody came.

I was not afraid that what Eman Petera called 'these people' might not come. But the arrangements had been so precise and so swiftly made that it was disconcerting that they should be late. I was keyed up and the delay threw me off balance.

I did not think it could be me that the men in the corner were waiting for. But clearly they were waiting for somebody for they kept glancing towards the door, and the one with his back to me slewed round at intervals and looked at the clock. Had Sonnenschein, I wondered, given them the wrong description? Unlikely but possible. Anyway it was worth investigating. When the clock showed twelve minutes past three I got up and walked across to the table in the corner.

'Excuse me,' I said, 'I think you might be expecting me.'

The three men rose to their feet and it was the one who had been sitting in the middle with his back to me who answered.

'What is your name?' he asked cautiously.

'Edita Zukermanova.'

'Ah!' His face lighted up. 'Then yes. We are the right people. We're waiting for your father.'

'My father's dead. He died a year ago. It's me you're waiting for.'

He looked bewildered.

'But . . .' He stopped short. 'Anyway, won't you sit down?'

The younger of the other two pulled out the only vacant chair, the one right in the corner so that I was sitting with the light on my face. I looked up and smiled my thanks. He was very dark. I thought he probably had Algerian blood. He must have been a few years older than me, say twenty-seven or twenty-eight. Although rather tall for a Frenchman he seemed a dwarf beside the one who had spoken to me. The latter was enormous, six foot four at least, and probably in his early forties.

The third man was older than his companions, a prominent nose jutted out from his lined, sun-tanned face. He had an air of authority but seemed content to listen while the middle-aged man talked to me.

'There must be a mistake,' he said. 'We were expecting a man.'

'No, really it is me you're expecting. Colonel Petera who has just joined you . . .'

'We have no Colonel Petera,' he broke in.

I was taken aback. 'Well, it was Mr Sonnenschein who fixed it up. You surely know Mr Sonnenschein.'

'Yes indeed. But he spoke to us of a man.'

'Then he got it wrong. But it can't matter. I mean the fact that I'm a woman can't make any difference. In fact it might be an advantage.'

The older man leaned forward and the others looked at him respectfully, waiting for him to speak. He asked me what I would like.

'A drink? Some coffee perhaps?'

'Could I have an ice-cream? A chocolate one.' Without turning round he raised his hand and beckoned to the waiter who flew to his side.

Nobody spoke while the ice was being fetched. None of these men had introduced themselves so I made up names for them. The elderly man I would call The Admiral for he looked like one. The very tall man I would call Le Grand and the third Le Petit.

I took a spoonful of the ice and turned to The Admiral.

'What will I have to do?' I asked.

He smiled. 'What do you want to do?'

'I want to be a spy of course. I speak perfect German and Italian so you must have some use for me. Besides you surely wouldn't have sent for me if you hadn't.'

He ignored my remark but he was smiling as he said, 'We don't call our people spies. They're secret agents. It's very dangerous. I really don't think it's a job for a young girl.'

'I'm over twenty-one,' I replied, indignantly. 'And as for being dangerous, so is crossing the street. I'm not afraid of anything.'

'Are you alone in France?'

'No. I'm with my mother. We live in Monte Carlo.'

'And what would your mother say?'

'She would never try to stop me doing anything I wanted to do.'

There was a pause. The men exchanged glances and The Admiral looked at his watch. If they got up I realized I would have no hope left. But they seemed to have good manners, so they would not leave until I had finished eating. I picked up my spoon and nibbled some more ice-cream. The Admiral spoke again.

'We never employ women,' he said patiently. 'Nothing to do with you, you are a very pretty and intelligent girl. But in our section we don't deal with women and that's all there is to it.'

The initiative was slipping away from me. I had to say something.

'But I speak perfect Italian and I have very good connections in Italy. For instance I know many officers.'

'Who?' The question was curt but not discourteous.

'Well Giuseppe Castellano for one. He's the colonel commanding the Heavy Artillery in Palermo.'

I sensed I had caught their interest.

'Giuseppe and I used to dance together when I was in Venice.

Perhaps we flirted a little. He was always asking me to visit him in Palermo.'

Now I was really holding my audience. I could almost see them prick up their ears. Le Grand and Le Petit bent their heads together and started whispering. The Admiral looked me straight in the eyes. It seemed that the name Castellano had some special significance for him.

I decided to press home my advantage.

'May I ask you a question?' I said.

He made a polite little gesture with his hands.

'Have you got a star?' I asked.

'A star?'

'Yes. Somebody outstanding in your section. Somebody really fantastic.'

The Admiral considered my question carefully.

'No, we are a team – we have very good team work – but I wouldn't call anybody a star.'

This was the crucial moment. There came back to me the image I had had on the bus, of an archer tautening his bowstring. I threw all my strength, all my willpower, all my personality into this one supreme effort. Now it was my turn to stare into The Admiral's eyes. Then I leaned forward and touched him gently on the shoulder.

'In that case I accept. *I* will be your star.'

He gulped; he could not find any words to counter my outrageous remark.

'All right,' he said hastily. 'We'll give it a try. But I'm sure that after two months or so you'll find a boy-friend, you'll become engaged, you'll marry him and you'll want to give up this work and be happy.'

I started to protest but he interrupted me.

'All right, all right. I said we'll give it a try.' He turned to Le Grand. 'Start her off.'

The Admiral rose to his feet and stretched out his hand.

'And when shall I have the pleasure of seeing you again?' I asked. He looked at me gravely.

'You won't see me. All your future dealings will be with one of these gentlemen. He will telephone you and make an appointment.'

All three shook hands with me and waited for me to leave.

As soon as I was through the door I broke into a run, up the steps of the Cristie Bar and along the Boulevard Victor Hugo. I was in a state of exaltation. It had all turned out exactly as I wanted it to, my dreams and hopes had become reality.

But on the long bus journey back to Monte Carlo reaction set in. I was exhausted, emotionally drained. I was sure I'd win. But what if they changed their minds? I did not even know how to find them again. Would I have to spend the rest of my life waiting for the sound of a telephone which never rang?

By the time I got back to the hotel I felt like a beaten dog. Mummy asked eagerly how I had got on.

'Oh all right. They're going to phone me,' I said dully.

My mother, thank God, was not a great questioner. That is one of the reasons why we got on so well. She left it at that.

I went to bed early, worn out and miserable.

When I awoke next morning all my confidence had returned. The excitement had built up and I hardly noticed the uphill walk to Monsieur Zimdin's apartment. There were no buses and I had come to dread the long trudge. But this morning my step was lighter, my back straighter. I was aware of being a woman. Soon, Monsieur Zimdin, I shall be rid of you, I said to myself.

Something of my new-found assurance must have communicated itself to Monsieur Zimdin because that morning when I said a cheerful good morning to him he handed me the letters instead of chucking them on the floor at my feet.

There was very little for me to do that day but Monsieur Zimdin always kept me there in case somebody who did not speak German should happen to call or telephone and I would be needed to act as interpreter. In the long hours when there was nothing to do I would often slip into the maid's room while she was out and rest on the bed. My back and legs never seemed to stop aching in Monte Carlo where I had to walk everywhere, uphill or downhill all the time.

So that afternoon, when I heard the door shut behind her as she set off to do the shopping I got up from the table where I was typing. There were only two more letters to do and there would be plenty of time for them later. Monsieur Zimdin would not release me for several hours yet.

I went to the maid's room, kicked off my shoes and stretched out thankfully on the bed. It was lovely to lie there, alone with my marvellous secret. For the first time since my father died I felt carefree, and happiness bubbled up inside me. I thought of some of the highspots of my life – my first dance, my first date, the first role in the school play, my first job. No, no, no. They may have seemed peaks of achievement, the ultimate in triumphant happiness – and perhaps at the time they were. Now they seemed trivial and childish. This was something far better. Far more important.

I slid off the bed and walked to the full-length looking glass on the wardrobe door.

Very carefully I examined my reflection, my hair, my face, my body, my legs, scrutinizing everything minutely. Then I tossed my head back and half closed my eyes – enigmatic and mysterious. I leaned forward and opened my eyes to their fullest extent – innocence. I cocked my head on one side and smiled – tantalizing. I tilted my chin – defiance.

Then I bent forward and addressed my reflection in a confidential whisper.

'*You are a spy!*'

As I walked out of the room and back to my typewriter I was humming happily.

Chapter 2

November 1938

For the next week I alternated between confidence and despair and it took all my mother's soothing wisdom to calm me as I veered from one extreme to the other. One evening I was feeling particularly low as I tramped back to the hotel – Monsieur Zimdin had been at his most inconsiderate – and I thought how awful it would be in the heat of summer to make this long walk with the sun beating back from the unrelenting paving stones. Even now, in the mild Mediterranean winter it was bad enough and I flung myself on to the bed weary in mind and body.

There was a knock on the door.

'A telephone call for Mademoiselle.'

I flew downstairs; a voice, which did not identify itself, instructed me to report to an address in Nice the following morning.

I raced upstairs, all fatigue forgotten. I grabbed my mother in my arms and together we did a little dance of joy.

'But what about Monsieur Zimdin? You just can't walk out on him without a word.'

'Oh him!' I thought for a moment. 'Mummy, you could go and make my apologies. Mummy, please!'

She nodded, smiling. She always did the awkward jobs for me, bless her.

My instructions had been precise – the street, the number, the floor, the room.

The tall man, whom I had privately nicknamed Le Grand, greeted me politely but without warmth. As one reciting a lesson he explained the terms of my employment. I would be paid three thousand francs a month – five hundred more than I had been getting from Monsieur Zimdin – and I would have the rank of

Sub-Lieutenant in the French Navy.

'That makes it seem much more professional,' I said. 'More than just being a spy, I mean.'

'A secret agent,' he corrected me.

I was surprised that Le Grand did not ask to see my passport or ask me about my background. As far as I was aware the only credentials presented to the Deuxième Bureau had been Colonel Petera's recommendations. When I asked Le Grand whether he wished to verify any facts about me he replied shortly.

'That has already been done.'

It was clear that questions were not welcome so I remained silent and looked round the room while listening to Le Grand. There was not much to see. It was the starkest room I had ever been in. Just a table and two hard chairs. There were a few lights such as are used in photographic studios, and that was all. Not a picture, not a carpet, not even a shade on the single bulb hanging from the ceiling. The room was as non-committal as Le Grand himself, totally impersonal.

'Be here at the same time tomorrow and we'll start your training.'

Colonel Petera came that evening to say good-bye.

I said to him, 'Something puzzles me. When I mentioned your name at the first interview the man said you didn't work for them. Was it just secrecy or is it true?'

'Perfectly true. You see, there are two sections. You're in the naval one and I'm in the military. Sonnenschein always tries to get people into the naval section if he can.'

'Why?'

'Because he gets five hundred francs more for them.'

Soon Eman left, it was an emotional parting, we all wept. It was worse for Mother than for me. I had my new career to occupy my mind. She had only her memories.

At first all my training took place in the bare room in Nice and Le Grand was the only member of the Deuxième Bureau I saw. He issued me with a camera and taught me how to use it, how to photograph documents, moving objects, things in shadow. This was before the days of electronic light meters, and shutter speeds and openings were matters for the photographer's own judgment.

I had always been interested in photography and was thrilled with this new camera. It was a Leica IIA, the very latest version of the first of the 'miniature' cameras, small enough to slip into one of the big handbags which were fashionable that winter. By modern standards it would be thought very bulky, five inches long, two and three quarter inches wide and weighing eighteen ounces.

It was only when I had thoroughly mastered the theory that Le Grand allowed me to take the camera out into the mountains behind Nice and demonstrate that I had learned my lessons.

Next came communications. I had expected elaborate cyphers but there was nothing like that. Everything was kept as simple as possible. I was told to preface my reports with one of three qualifications. The first, 'I hear', meant that it was just a rumour. 'I see' meant that the information had come from a reliable source. The highest category, 'I know', was to be used only when the agent was absolutely convinced of the complete truth and accuracy of the report.

When Le Grand told me about writing with invisible ink and what to use I could hardly believe it.

'But that's what we used to do at school! Is that all?'

The 'ink' was either lemon juice or powdered aspirin mixed with water. You wrote on a very rough sort of paper and held it slanting to the light so that you could see what you were writing. In seconds it would dry and become invisible. To make it legible all that was needed was to heat it with an iron or toast it in front of a fire.

Le Grand patiently explained that as the 'invisible' writing could so easily be detected it was of the greatest importance that nobody except the recipient should suspect that it existed. It must, therefore, be contained between the lines of an ordinary letter, a letter so apparently genuine that it would never occur to anybody to doubt its innocence.

In those days there were no ballpoints and everybody wrote with fountain pens. I would need two, one with ordinary ink, and the other ostensibly spare and unused, for the lemon juice. Le Grand emphasized that I must always wash and rinse it thoroughly after using it so that if my belongings should be searched no trace of the invisible ink would be found.

Invisible ink would be used only for long reports. For short reports the method was even simpler. They would be written microscopically on a postcard and completely covered by the stamp. I found this a particularly tiresome thing to do. My normal writing is large and sprawling. In addition I am astigmatic so it is impossible for me to see sharp outlines.

Le Grand questioned me closely about my memory and seemed satisfied when I told him that I had started to train to be an actress and that I knew twenty parts by heart. Memory, he warned me, was an agent's most important piece of equipment.

'Never write anything down. If you're caught you have a chance of getting away with it if they don't find anything. But if you've got something written down . . .'

Throughout our time in Monte Carlo my mother and I had been living in a three-star hotel, not because we could afford it but because we couldn't afford not to. It was essential to give the impression of having money. Monte Carlo was full of refugees from Nazi tyranny and the authorities were very firm with any whom they believed to be without visible means of support. Now that I had perfectly legally obtained employment (though naturally I could never disclose its nature), it was quite safe for us to move to some cheaper hotel.

The one we found – the Hotel de la Poste – had a very kind owner, a Czech, who was also a very good cook. He offered us two tiny rooms on the fourth floor of his shabby little hotel. There was no lift, but the rooms had the bare essentials. One had a gas ring and the other had a washbasin so we were able to cook meals for ourselves and wash up afterwards.

The atmosphere which Mummy managed to create was amazing. She, who had been accustomed to a busy social life in Vienna, entertaining in her big flat surrounded by her beautiful belongings, turned those two little rooms into a home. Her vivid personality overcame all the sorrows, all the worries. She manufactured happiness.

I was proud of my mother, with her beauty, her gaiety; most of all I loved it when people took her for my elder sister. She had a way of entering into things with me, and making it all fun. She was helpful, too, in my training. In order to sharpen my memory we used to sit for hours outside cafés watching the traffic. I would try to memorize the make of a passing car, its colour, the number of its occupants and the registration number.

Mother would write down all the particulars and in the evening she would examine me on them. At first I could get only one or two right but after several weeks I was able to reel off twelve or fourteen without a fault. I remembered numbers by relating the figures to something personal – the date of a friend's birthday, my size in shoes, the distance between two places I knew well.

At last Le Grand was satisfied that I was fit to be sent on a simple mission. I was to go to San Remo and report the names of the ships of the Italian Navy in harbour there. It wouldn't, he explained, require much initiative because all the sailors had their ships' names on their hatbands. I was disappointed at being given a task so easy as to be derisory and I wondered whether I was going to be watched to see how I behaved myself. Anyway I went to San Remo, read the hatbands and duly recorded my findings on the corner of a postcard, then I covered it with a stamp and waited to be told to come home.

After about ten days I received a postcard inviting me to a fictitious party and thankfully returned to Monte Carlo, travelling on the hard wooden seats of the third class. The Deuxième Bureau allowed its agents second class fares but I preferred to put up with the discomfort and supplement my small income with the difference in the travel allowance. It was, however, difficult not to be out of pocket on hotel expenses because the permitted rate was so small.

'We are not rich,' Le Grand announced bleakly. 'Nor are we a charity.'

It was only a few days after my return from San Remo that I was called to Nice. This time it was not Le Grand who was waiting for me in the stark room but Le Petit. Indeed now that my training was finished I was never to see Le Grand again. He slipped out of my life as quietly and colourlessly as he had entered it.

Le Petit was a man of a totally different stamp, enthusiastic and friendly. His height and his bright dark eyes might have made him physically attractive but I did not find him so. For his part he was deeply in love with his wife and I very much doubt if he was ever physically aware of anyone else. We soon established an easy uncomplicated brother-sister relationship.

My new task was again to report on ships but this time in Sicily. Le Petit explained that it was important to the Bureau to know the direction of the potential naval thrust in the Mediterranean – whether westward against France or eastward against the British bases. I was to start in Palermo and then go to Catania. I should, I was told, look up Giuseppe Castellano.

'Oh yes,' I said. 'I thought The Admiral seemed interested in him.'

'The Admiral?' said Le Petit sharply. 'Why do you call him that?'

'Well, because he looks like one. I don't know his name.'

'Oh I see. Well, anyhow, try and find out Colonel Castellano's views – when he thinks the war will come, what course he expects it to take. Things like that.'

It all sounded rather vague but tremendously exciting. I might, I realized, be able to do something thoroughly worthwhile. I felt that Eman Petera would, if he had known, have been very proud that I had been entrusted with such an important mission.

I tried to tell myself that I was motivated by the same high sense of patriotism as he was. But it was not so. The adventure was the attraction, not the thought of doing something for Czechoslovakia. But it is also true that the wider cause of freedom held a great appeal and I was thankful for the opportunity to do something against Hitler. But not even that would have made me quite so eager to throw myself into danger. No, I had to admit it – it was the adventure which really counted.

So far as patriotic duty was concerned it was France which meant far more to me than Czechoslovakia. I liked the French, I admired their spirit, the Marseillaise never failed to sweep me along on a wave of emotion. I had been educated in Switzerland and had spoken French for as long as I could remember, I seemed to fit naturally into the French way of life and thought. With my cosmopolitan upbringing I had never had a homeland and France was, I felt, the country where I could put down roots.

These were the thoughts which filled my mind as the train rumbled down to Naples. I was so keyed up by the sense of adventure that I hardly noticed the beauty of the country through which we passed; even Naples and its Bay made little impact, so impatient was I to get to my work.

But when I arrived in Palermo it was brought home to me that

I must proceed very cautiously and slowly indeed. A girl travelling alone was both conspicuous and suspect, particularly one like myself who was so obviously a foreigner, with my lighter skin and hair. Even my clothes, thin and summery in gay colours were in marked contrast to the Sicilian black. The conventions about wearing mourning were very strict in Sicily – so many years for a husband, so many years for a father, a mother, a brother, a sister, a child. The death of even quite a distant relation would plunge a Sicilian woman into black so that very few girls left their teens before their light dresses had to be put away.

The conventions of behaviour were equally rigid. Only prostitutes walked unaccompanied in the streets. The manager of the hotel made a sour face when he saw me booking in. It was the Excelsior, Palermo's best hotel. In spite of my meagre boarding allowance I thought it essential to be staying at a good hotel because otherwise Giuseppe Castellano would find it strange that if I could not comfortably afford it, I should have taken the trouble to come to Sicily for a holiday. To tell the truth I had exaggerated my friendship with him to impress The Admiral. It was hardly more than a casual acquaintanceship – certainly not enough to justify a special journey. I decided, therefore, to wait several days before calling on him.

However, it was imperative that I find an escort of some sort. It would be courting disaster for me to prowl round the docks by myself. Fortunately one Italian custom had penetrated the hard crust of Sicily's code of behaviour and that was that it was considered perfectly proper for a man to address a woman without being introduced, provided always that the surroundings were highly respectable. Consequently I was able to enter into conversation when a young man spoke to me in the lounge of the hotel. He was wearing the uniform of a lieutenant in the Italian army and not only would he be good 'cover' for me but he might let slip some interesting information. When he asked me to go swimming with him at Mondello the next afternoon I readily agreed.

He had a rather grand car and when I remarked on it he explained that one of his senior officers had lent it to him for his leave. It was a pity, he said, that he had to return to his regiment next day. I thought it was a pity, too. I would have to find another escort.

We had to make a detour because the direct road to Mondello ran through a prohibited military zone but even so there was plenty of time for us to lie on the beach, swim, and lie on the beach again. If only my companion had been less boring! Finally he ran out of cigarettes so we drove back to Palermo. On the way he pulled up at a tobacconist and I waited for him in the car. As he closed the door I noticed the corner of a map sticking out of the pocket. Probably, I thought, it would be a street guide to Palermo and possibly it would give more detail than maps readily available in France. I slipped it into my bag, just in case. I had no twinge of conscience. My job was to gather information and the loss could hardly be a serious one for the young lieutenant. I doubted if he would even notice but if he did he could always get another map from his regiment.

It was a relief to say good-bye to him but there still remained the problem of finding an escort. I asked the hall porter if there were any places in Palermo where they had *thé dansant* – the afternoon dancing which was then a craze all over Europe. He was shocked at the suggestion that there should be such a thing in Sicily and then grudgingly admitted that at the Villa Igea they did have dancing 'for foreigners'.

For a Sicilian even Italians from the mainland were foreigners, but as far as I could tell all the people at the Villa Igea were Sicilian. There was a big ballroom and at tables round the edge sat girls, each accompanied by an older woman. A young man would go up to the table, bow, and ask the chaperone's permission to dance with the girl. I felt uncomfortably aware of being alone, and I was delighted when a young man came up to the table where I was sitting.

Antonio Fici had a profile like an ancient Roman coin and although he was pure Sicilian he had blue eyes. He was about my own age and was, he told me, studying chemistry in order to go into the family business in Marsala. His father was sitting at their table. He introduced me to his father who must have approved of me because when it was time to go he agreed to Antonio borrowing the car to take me back to the hotel.

When we got to the Excelsior he asked diffidently whether we might meet again. I was delighted. Not only would he be a companion for me to be seen with but he would be a most agreeable one. For the next few days, before his studies began again, we were inseparable. At first I asked him to come with me to visit the docks – I had to go for several days running to see if the same ships were still there – but very soon we walked all round Palermo. He was proud of his city and liked showing it to me. As for me, I just liked being with him.

The friendship ripened like a fruit in the hot Sicilian sunshine. In a very short time we were walking hand-in-hand, students in love. Antonio would sigh and say 'If only I had finished my studies . . .' or 'if only you didn't live so far away'. If only . . . But under my breath all I could say was 'If only there were not a war coming. If only our countries could be on the same side.' For me the war had already begun.

I told Antonio that I had promised to go and see Colonel Castellano, and one morning I announced that I intended to go that afternoon. I had been in Palermo long enough to satisfy Castellano – he would realize, should he enquire, that I had not come there specially to see him. I have always had an intuitive feeling about timing. I wait until I have this inner certainty that the time is right – now I felt that yesterday would have been too early, and that tomorrow would be too late.

'I was hoping we could spend the afternoon together. You see, I've got a lecture this evening,' Antonio said.

'Never mind. I shan't be very long and we'll have an hour or two before your lecture. We can go to our trees.'

The hall porter was not surprised when I asked him the whereabouts of the barracks. Military installations might be highly secret but everybody knew and admired the massive barracks in the pompous neo-Roman style in which Mussolini had caused buildings to spring up all over the Italian Empire. It was therefore quite natural that I should want to see one of the sights of Palermo. I would find the barracks, the porter said, on the flat land beside the airfield, not very far away.

The two carabinieri who were lolling beside the imposing gates eyed me speculatively as I approached but they stiffened to attention and their manner changed when I enquired for their colonel. Another soldier was summoned to show me the way and I set off in a flurry of salutes. They probably thought I was Giuseppe's niece.

There was no answer to the tap on the door bearing Colonel Castellano's name so the soldier opened it and left me there, muttering something about finding the colonel. It was a large room with a huge desk covered with papers. I longed to see what they were – what a scoop it would be if I could take photographs of all those secret documents! But I did not dare. Giuseppe might come in at any moment and I could not risk being found near the desk. I strolled over to the wide window. It looked out on the gunpark, with the airfield beyond. Rows and rows of guns were drawn up. So that was what 'Heavy Artillery' looked like. I must count them so that I could tell Le Petit. But I could imagine him asking all sorts of technical questions which I would never be able to answer. The best thing I could do would be to photograph them so that he could see for himself. Not that army guns were likely to be of much interest to our naval Intelligence department.

I took out the Leica, set the shutter speed and began to take photographs. If Colonel Castellano caught me doing it I would be all innocence, explaining that it was a fine view which anybody would like to see a picture of, even though it was rather spoilt by those silly old guns.

But I was not disturbed. I finished the film and slipped the camera back into my bag. I was at the end of the room farthest from both the desk and the window when Colonel Castellano came in.

For a moment he did not recognize me. It was obvious that he was indignant and outraged at finding me in his office. All this was reflected in his face.

I put on my most innocent expression.

'Well, here I am. You always told me to come and see you if I happened to be in Palermo,' I said brightly.

'Yes, yes,' he replied without any great enthusiasm. 'But you should have written, or at least telephoned. You oughtn't to have come here, to the barracks.'

He was very clearly much put out. But whether it was fear or embarrassment I could not tell. He did not ask me how long I

29

was going to stay in Palermo, or even where I was staying. He was obviously eager to get rid of me. And I was eager to go.

I went back to the Excelsior, bitterly regretting that I had ever mentioned the name of Colonel Giuseppe Castellano to The Admiral. I could not disguise from myself that my first real mission had been a failure.

Chapter 3

April 1939

After my unpleasant experience at the barracks I was even more than usually delighted to see Antonio. We went to 'our trees', two large and ancient trees, famous in Palermo because they form a sort of whispering gallery. Although they are some distance apart if you put your lips to one and whispered, what you said could be heard quite clearly by someone with their ear to the other tree. Antonio and I loved this arboreal telephone and we would spend hours whispering to each other. That afternoon we were completely absorbed, and took no heed of time. Suddenly I happened to hear a clock strike.

'Goodness! You'll be late for your lecture.'

Antonio wanted to escort me back to the hotel but I insisted that he should go straight to his class. As I was walking back alone a car drew up beside me.

'Can I give you a lift?' asked the young man at the wheel.

'But I don't know you,' I exclaimed.

'Oh yes you do. I'm Mario Grandi. I'm staying at the Excelsior, the same as you. Do get in. Are you going there now?'

I dimly remembered seeing him in the hotel and I was glad to be saved a long walk – already in April it was getting hot in Palermo.

Mario began telling me about the car. It was new, a present from his father, a Lancia Aprilia.

'Of course,' said Mario, 'really to see how good its performance is you need to try it on a mountain road. How about going up above Palermo for half an hour?'

I hesitated. I was due to leave for Catania early next morning and I wanted an early night. On the other hand I made it a rule always to take advantage of any opportunity offered for gaining information. It was unlikely that I would see anything of interest to the Deuxième Bureau but I just might. So, I decided to accept Mario's suggestion. It never entered my head to suspect his motives. Sicilians had a great respect for women and I thought I should be perfectly safe.

I know nothing about cars but even I could see that the Lancia went very fast up the winding mountain road and I made suitably complimentary noises. I soon realized that there was nothing of interest from an espionage point of view, and when we stopped at the top of the pass to look down on the lights of Palermo I asked Mario to turn round and go back. He nodded, but when he set off and I saw that he was heading away from Palermo I became a little uneasy, and repeated my request to be taken back to the hotel. He laughed and stopped the car.

'Give me a kiss,' he demanded.

I was surprised, but not frightened. I did not like him much and I refused. He put his hand on my knee.

'Look,' I said. 'If you don't leave me alone I'll get out of the car.'

He only laughed and made another grab.

This would have made me angry at any time and place. But late at night, in those lonely mountains, fear lent a spur to my anger. I was in a towering rage as I jumped out of the car and slammed the door. I turned round to scream defiance at Mario but he had already started the engine and with a jerk he spun the car round in a tight turn, pebbles at the side of the road scattering from under the wheels. Savagely accelerating the Lancia headed back towards Palermo. I stood, watching unbelievingly.

As the sound of the engine died away the darkness pressed in on me, enfolding me like a black velvet cloak.

How far was I from Palermo? Ten miles, twenty? Even in the city of Palermo traffic was sparse in 1939. The chances of a car passing this godforsaken spot at this hour were minimal. I had made a fool of myself on an impressive scale.

I knew I could not walk all the way. So it was not worth walking at all. For my walks with Antonio I always wore comfortable sandals. But as it happened there had not been time to change after returning from the barracks and I was still wearing the smart clothes I had put on – abortively – to impress Colonel

Castellano. I was determined to save something from the wreck of that disastrous day even if it was only my beautiful high-heeled shoes and one of my very few remaining pairs of sheer silk stockings.

I sat down in the dust – there was nowhere else to sit – to wait for morning.

What a fool I had been! How The Admiral and Le Petit would laugh if they knew that the agent who had proclaimed herself to be their star was squatting in the middle of nowhere, in the middle of the night, and all because she did not know how to handle an amorous boy not yet out of his teens!

I was roused by the rattling of an ancient truck firing on three cylinders. Scarcely waiting to brush the dust from my skirt, I ran into the middle of the road and waved frantically as the glimmering yellow headlights wobbled slowly towards me.

The driver, all dark skin, white teeth, and concern, leaned from his rickety cab, to ask me a string of questions in the harsh accent of a Sicilian peasant. When he heard my story he was horrified. I must of course come with him to his village. Alas, to take me to Palermo was impossible. He himself was hastening home to his wife who had, by God's mercy, this very evening been delivered of a thriving baby boy, the image, so the message said, of his father.

To argue or to bribe would have been futile. I clambered into the smelly cab and jolted away to the primitive cottage where a tremendous birthday party was in progress. I shook hands with everyone, I kissed the baby, I held the hand of the mother, a young girl whose only wish was to be left in peace with her infant and her proud, clumsy husband. Nobody asked me anything. They accepted me, unquestioningly, for it was the right of all the world to celebrate such an important event. The clouds of war were rolling remorselessly towards the remotest parts of Europe, of the world, and yet these peasants, rejoicing, like so many characters in a Dutch painting, were gloriously unaware of Hitler, of Beneš, of Chamberlain, of Daladier. Perhaps they had heard of Mussolini, a great man certainly but remote, living on the mainland like the Pope.

The dark roughness of the local wine, the compelling tang of the goat's milk cheese, the hunk of crisply fresh bread, the sweaty peasant smell, here was life at its simple best, age-old and ageless and presently concerned with an atavistic celebration of its continuance. A far cry indeed from sophistication, from politics, from the Nazis, the Fascists, the Deuxième Bureau and from Monte Carlo.

I shook the euphoria from my eyes and told anybody who would listen that I *had to* get back to Palermo. Somebody did. The blacksmith had a car, yes a car. He would drive me to Palermo. Gladly. All it would cost me would be three hundred lire.

By the time the rattling, swaying vehicle had deposited me at the hotel I was completely exhausted. And when the manager, who happened to be passing through the hall, spoke to me I recklessly poured out the whole story.

He was horrified. That a Sicilian should treat a woman – and a visitor at that – in such a way was shocking. I must, he urged, report the matter to the police. That, of course, was the last thing I wanted to do. I begged the manager to let the matter drop except that I thought that Mario Grandi should pay the three hundred lire – I would have a very thin time in Catania if I did not get them back.

There was only one train a day to Catania and I had already missed it. Antonio was at his lectures and, with nothing to do, I hung about the hotel. I was in the hall when Mario came in. Immediately the hall porter and the indignant manager closed in upon him and demanded that he should refund the three hundred lire.

Mario dismissed their demands contemptuously. 'She's not worth it. Anyway, she's only a foreigner.' He stalked away.

I had been put in a hideous position. The insult was so great that if I ignored it the manager would at once suspect that I had something to hide. And I desperately needed the three hundred lire. I reported the incident at the police station.

Next day I moved to Catania, furious with myself for having mixed up my mission with a silly escapade which had nothing to do with it. Catania was a dreary place, huddling under the black bulk of Mount Etna. One would have to be in a very romantic mood to find beauty in Catania. I was not.

If I, a woman travelling alone, had been conspicuous in Palermo, in provincial Catania I was a thousand times more so. The hotel was swarming with men in uniform – the black shirts of the Fascists were predominant but there were officers of all three services. And if I entered the dining room or the bar they would all immediately stop talking and turn to look at me. It was the same in the street, on my way to and from the docks. I could feel people staring at my back, speculating about me.

Gradually I came to the conclusion that my sense of unease was due to something more specific than the universal curiosity I was arousing. I became convinced that I was under observation. My suspicions were heightened when an elderly man arrived at the hotel. He spoke to me often and I kept seeing him in town. He was friendly and rather inquisitive, but I noticed he never paid me a compliment. Paying compliments to women is so much a custom in Italy and Sicily that it only assumes significance by its absence.

I determined to find out whether I really was being observed. I opened my suitcase and laid three hairs across its forward edge. Then I closed the lid very slowly and gently. I had to try several times before I managed to close it without disturbing the hairs but after a number of experiments I was satisfied that it would be impossible for anybody to open the case without dislodging them. I closed the lid once more, making quite sure that the hairs were in position. I did not lock the case. Then I went down to the docks to see if there had been any change in the shipping since the previous day.

When I got back to the room there was no sign of the hairs. So my case had been searched and my suspicions confirmed.

I was not specially worried. In the summer of 1939 war fever was rapidly mounting and it was quite likely that the police would attempt to screen any foreign visitor to Sicily as a routine matter. The other possibilities were more sinister. The Rome-Berlin Axis, the alliance between Nazis and Fascists had a much murkier side than that which the world was allowed to see. The Germans, the dominant partner in this unholy marriage, spied on the Italians and the Italians spied on each other. I would have felt almost left out of it if nobody had spied upon me.

There was nothing even remotely incriminating in my suitcase. The Leica, the film I had taken in the barracks, and the map I had stolen were all in the bag which never left my side. The only thing in the case which had any connection with espionage was the small electric iron that I used to heat the

35

letters from the Bureau so as to bring out the message written in invisible ink. But before the invention of drip-dry materials every woman took a portable iron in her luggage – it would have been strange if I had not had one. None of my possessions could have betrayed me.

Nevertheless the secret police forces were not renowned for their restraint and although no shred of evidence could be produced against me I had no wish to tangle with either the German Gestapo or the Italian OVRA.* Their weapons were different – the German cudgel, the Italian rapier – but they were equally deadly. I decided to leave Sicily as soon as I could. The next train to Palermo was not until the following morning and, to calm my impatience, I went for a last walk in Catania – though I was careful to keep well away from the docks.

As I re-entered the hotel and passed the porter's desk he nodded quickly at two men who had been standing in the shadow. As they stepped forward I saw that they wore police uniform.

'Mademoiselle Edita Zukermanova?'

In the split second before I replied a whole battery of questions flashed through my mind. Had I left something in the suitcase after all? Had my letters been intercepted and tested for invisible ink? Had the officer whose map I stole traced me?

'Yes,' I answered with a rising inflexion. I hoped it sounded polite and surprised.

'We must ask you to return to Palermo to give evidence in the case of Mario Grandi.'

My reaction was instinctive and immediate. *You must not show relief* I told myself.

'It is a shame to break into your holiday,' remarked the elder police officer. Kind man.

'Oh it doesn't matter a bit. Actually you aren't. I was going back to Palermo tomorrow in any case.'

Mario Grandi! I had entirely forgotten about him, erased the shaming and distasteful memory of that idiotic episode from my mind.

A few more polite sentences and the policemen left. I hoped

* Organizzazione Volontaria Repressione Antifascismo.

36

my knees were not visibly shaking as I tried to stroll nonchalantly across the hall.

'Excuse me, miss.'

But this time it was only the porter, handing me a letter. Somebody called Maurice was writing passionate endearments. I plugged in my electric iron and passed it over the rough paper, watching the brown letters spring into view between the black lines.

'Italian Air Force establishment changed yesterday. Discover new number planes in squadron. Seven or nine. Important. Urgent.'

I suppose it was the last word which made me think that the information must be gathered immediately, before I took the train next day. In fact it would have been easier in Palermo where it was obvious that I would be staying for several days until the ludicrous Mario incident was finally disposed of. Perhaps I was still in a state of shock from the confrontation with the police. I was not reasoning clearly.

I went down to the bar.

I looked round for an Air Force officer. It was not difficult. There was a handsome lieutenant. I looked at him. He looked at me. I looked away. He went on looking. I looked again and smiled. He offered me a drink, a drive.

'Not up Mount Etna.' I had Mario in mind.

He laughed. 'Of course not. Perhaps to the beach. It is very romantic in the moonlight.'

It was. When he kissed me I did not resist. It would not go beyond a little cuddling. He was a nice young man and nice young men did not go beyond a little cuddling with girls they had known for half an hour. Not in 1939.

He murmured compliments – rather obvious compliments. I remained silent, wanting to get it over as quickly as I could. His breathing quickened, his caresses became more purposeful. I judged that the moment for which I had been waiting, when his brain would not be working too clearly, was imminent.

'How many planes in your squadron? Seven or nine?'

'Nine.' He spoke absently, sweetly and caressingly. Then suddenly he drew away from me.

'Why?' he demanded. 'Why did you ask that? Why do you want to know?'

37

A startled face, very close to mine, stared at me in the moonlight.

'Because I'm a member of the French Deuxième Bureau. We need this information.'

The startled face showed fear.

'That's certainly not true.'

Without another word he started the car and in silence we drove back to the hotel.

My answer had been instinctive, automatic, without thought. A reflex response to danger. If I had carefully worked out a reply it would not have been so effective. The truth is seldom believed. If by some wild chance the officer had believed me I would have laughed in his face. 'You must be nuts,' I would have said. 'It was a joke. Surely you don't think I would admit to being a member of the French Deuxième Bureau if I really were?'

With my slight German accent he probably thought I was working for the Nazi counter-espionage, assessing his security rating. I could even have been working for his own country, testing morale.

I am afraid that nice, handsome young officer must have spent some very anxious days.

'Mario Grandi is under arrest,' the *juge d'instruction** told me. I was astonished. It seemed unnecessarily severe.

'Yes indeed,' he went on. 'This is a very grave charge and if he is proved guilty he will serve a long prison sentence. A very long sentence.'

'Oh but must that happen? I mean, can't the charge be dropped?'

'It isn't as easy as that. You see, you are a Czech citizen and your country is under German protection.'

I bit my tongue to hold back the scornful denial.

'The Germans are allies of Italy. So we do not want to disoblige them. A pity for Mario Grandi,' he sighed. 'A young man of good family, respected in Sicily. An only son, too. And besides, he is willing to refund your three hundred lire.'

---

* There is no precise equivalent to *juge d'instruction* in British Law. The nearest translation is 'examining magistrate'.

'Well that's fine. Then we can forget the whole thing.'

'It's not as easy as that,' the *juge* repeated. 'You see, the German consul has interested himself in the case. He's looking forward to making an example of this young man.'

I was desperate. The publicity would be appalling. I had visions of having to come back to Palermo to attend the trial. The Deuxième Bureau would chuck me out and who could blame them? The only thing I could do was to appeal to the German consul and I was not very good at appealing to Germans.

I found him standing next to his CD car beside the harbour, waiting to welcome a guest. He was none too pleased to be interrupted but I made him listen to me. I used every argument I could think of – I minimized the incident, I said it would be undignified for a citizen of the great German Reich to pursue so vindictively a stupid little boy who had lost his head, I told him my parents would be shocked, that I wanted to go back to Vienna. He listened with an ill grace and it was only as the ship he was due to meet entered the harbour that he gave me his full attention.

'These Sicilians admire us Germans so much,' I said, 'and of course they're a little afraid of us. I think they would regard an act of clemency as a demonstration not only of our goodwill but of our greatness that we, with all our power, can still show mercy.'

'There is something in what you say,' he agreed grudgingly. 'All right. I will have the case quashed.'

I made a mental note of the name of the ship he was meeting and withdrew.

But I never did get my three hundred lire back.

The contrast between the luxury of the large and gracious Hotel Excelsior and the two tiny rooms up four flights of stairs at the Hotel de la Poste could not have been more extreme. But what a joy it was to be back in Mummy's happiness factory! I hoped I would never see Palermo or Catania or indeed any part of Sicily again.

I telephoned the Deuxième Bureau and was told to report in Nice not to the stark room, but to a hotel. The Hotel Alsace-Lorraine, 3, rue Alsace-Lorraine, was small but very clean and

39

comfortable. As soon as I saw the proprietress, Madame Gauthier, sitting behind a table in the narrow hall, I recognized that her standards would be high. Strikingly handsome and dressed most elegantly she had an air of quiet competence. Without asking any questions she showed me into a bedroom – just like any other bedroom in the hotel – where I was joined ten minutes later by Le Petit. He said that we would always meet there in future, arriving and leaving separately. The advantage of a hotel was that people were always going in and out and we could be less conspicuous than we would if we were meeting regularly at a private house.

He told me that my reports on the shipping had been satisfactory and then asked me about Colonel Castellano. He listened impassively as I described the disastrous interview, and dismissed my apologies with a shrug.

'May I have the film?' he enquired.

I produced it from my bag. 'Oh and one other thing. I found this map in a car. I don't expect it's any use but I thought I'd better bring it. It's such a small scale you can hardly read it.'

He glanced at it. 'It's a copy of a big one, much reduced. I agree it's probably no good to us but you did quite right to bring it. And now go and rest for three or four days before your next mission.'

It was difficult to know what he thought. He had been polite enough, had complimented me on my shipping reports, he had concealed any disappointment he may have felt over the Castellano affair. Nevertheless I had an uneasy feeling that he considered the whole thing a waste of time and money.

And when he telephoned, not three or four days later but the next morning, I thought he was summoning me to Nice to tell me that my services were no longer required.

But when I entered the room at the Alsace-Lorraine I found a very different Le Petit from the previous day. He welcomed me with a broad grin, his huge round eyes sparkling like traffic lights. He was almost dancing with excitement.

'Marvellous!' he said. 'That film you took in the gun park. Tells us a lot. We can see from the way the guns are lined up how the batteries are divided into troops in the new establishment. And best of all it shows the defences of the airfield. Our experts can deduce the principle of the defence – that'll apply to all Italian airfields – the pictures are so sharp we can tell the calibre of the guns and everything.'

I had learned enough about espionage to know the value of silence. So I did not say that, with my defective eyesight, I had not even seen the defences of the airfield let alone deliberately photographed them.

Chapter 4

Even though the photographing of the airfield defences had been a happy accident I had at least penetrated to one of the very few places which overlooked the airfield so I allowed myself some satisfaction. There was more to follow.

'Come as quickly as you can,' Le Petit commanded, when he telephoned later the same day. In those circumstances a character in any of the spy novels I had read would have leaped into his waiting Bugatti, or, if of an earlier generation, ordered a special train. But this was real life and I took the bus.

'That map you pinched. It's absolutely fantastic. We've had it photographed and blown up. It's a strategic map – marked with all the defence areas of Sicily, and, better still, it's got all the dumps and stores marked – fuel, ammunition, food. Fantastic!'

It was a wonderful moment. With the film I had tasted success. With the map I was rolling it round my tongue. Le Petit brought me down to earth with a bang.

'We want you to go back to Palermo at once.'

I was horrified. 'But that's impossible. I'm under suspicion already. And you can have no idea how conspicuous a girl on her own is in Sicily. I stick out like a sore thumb.'

Le Petit thought for a moment. 'Why not take your mother with you?'

This seemed a good idea. To return to Sicily was an order and naval officers did not disobey orders. Having my mother with me would quieten suspicions about me and it would not place her in any danger.

I do not think she liked the idea much but she never objected to anything which she thought was good for me, so off we went on the long journey to Rome, to Naples, then to Palermo.

'At least,' my mother said, 'you'll be able to see Antonio again.' I always told her about my boy-friends.

'No.' I shook my head. I had made up my mind that I would not tell Antonio that I was returning to Sicily. I was afraid of becoming too much attached to him.

I had a mission to perform, a job to do, and it would require all my concentration. I was aware that a woman even more than a man is a prey to her emotions and I was determined that nothing would be allowed to deflect me from my purpose. A horse in a field can toss its head and kick up its heels as much as it likes. But once it is harnessed it must conform to a rigid discipline. My mission was my harness.

It would have been madness to return to the Excelsior, even if we could have afforded to. On my previous visit I had noticed a charming little pensione on the outskirts of the city. It had a garden so at least it looked cooler than the bustling city centre though in fact it was far too hot for us ever to sit out.

Le Petit had warned me that I would probably have to stay in Sicily for several weeks if not months and he had arranged for my salary to be sent to me in Italian currency. The Deuxième Bureau had a system of carriers – men who had lived all their lives in the high mountains and who knew the secret ways across the frontier between Italy and France, but the money for agents working in Italy was distributed from a centre within that country.

Every morning we would take a walk down to the docks to note the movements of shipping. The heat from the unyielding paving stones scorched through the soles of our sandals and, quite apart from the discomfort, it was ruination to our stockings. Impossible to adopt the sensible course of going bare-legged – nothing would more surely have drawn attention to us. The stern conventions of Sicily were at least fifty years behind the rest of Europe – women without stockings? Unthinkable.

The afternoons we spent lying on our beds, gasping for breath. We had to keep our bodies covered with the sheets because of the flies. Oh the horror of those Sicilian flies! They were like a rippling black cloth spread on everything; our hands, our hair, our clothes – all were covered with them. We had to wave a hand over our plates while we were eating, and to brush away the flies which settled on our lips.

The cost of new stockings made a considerable hole in our slender budget and I worked out that we would have just enough money to last until the first monthly payment arrived. Punctually, on the day it was due, a parcel came for me. I took off the paper carefully so as not to tear any notes there might be folded into it. There were none.

The parcel contained a box of chocolates.

'The money must be inside the box,' I said.

'I doubt it,' Mummy replied. 'Look, you can see it's never been opened. That ribbon has never been untied.'

'That simply shows how clever my people are,' I said proudly. 'Now just you watch.' I opened the box and examined the packing, layer by layer. No money. I even cut each chocolate in half. No money.

As I sat, near to tears, my hands covered in melted chocolate and flies, she summed up the situation.

'Nobody but an idiot would send chocolates in this heat, money or no money.'

It was inconvenient but not disastrous. I had a ring which I pawned and I wrote to the Deuxième Bureau and told them what had happened. I was confident that everything would be all right in a few days.

Weeks went by and still the money did not come. I pawned another ring and did not worry too much. I could not imagine that the Deuxième Bureau would be any less loyal to me than I to them. My mother took a less sanguine view. I saw things as I wanted them to be. She saw them as they were.

I did not mind having to go to the pawnshop. It was not the first time and there was nothing terrible about it. It is only when you have nothing left to pawn to pay the interest on what is already in, that the time has come to worry.

The only humiliating thing was having to explain to the owner of the pensione that we could not pay his bill until the money arrived. He was kind and understanding, and I was grateful that he believed my assurance that the money would turn up eventually.

Although Mother was marvellous 'cover' I needed somebody else as well, a boy-friend. All the girls in Sicily had boy-friends and I was conspicuous without one. That was the sole reason. There is a popular myth that female secret agents lure enemy officers into bed to extract secrets from them on the pillow. Nothing could be farther from the truth. The time to extract the secrets is during the stage when the officer is trying to persuade the agent to get into bed. When he is showing off, making himself as interesting as he can, demonstrating his importance. If he does manage to have intercourse with her one of two things happens. Either he loses interest and she never gets any more information from him. Or he falls in love with her and is always hanging round, hampering and hindering her work.

In fact most young men would probably not have allowed themselves to be lured in any case. I doubt, for example, if the officer from whose car I had taken the map – or even Mario Grandi – would have come to bed with me if I had offered. Before the invention of the Pill, contraception was unreliable and the young were haunted by the risk of pregnancy outside wedlock, with all the social and financial consequences it entailed. That is not to say that the young men of the day were totally frustrated. They regularly indulged in the preliminary kissing, cuddling, caressing. Occasionally it led to a solitary orgasm. But rarely to sex with the woman.

It was not difficult to find an escort even though I was determined to reject any who did not possess a car – the ache in my feet had become a preoccupation.

I found a very nice Army lieutenant. Sadly, all the men I picked up in this cold-blooded way were nice. Otherwise they could not have fallen into the trap.

He took me out to dinner several times – sometimes he took my mother – and one day he asked us to go with him to swim at Mondello. In the fierce heat of Palermo no prospect could have been more attractive, and I accepted eagerly. Mother was not feeling well so she declined.

The lieutenant's car was old and we had to raise our voices to be heard above the roar and clatter of the engine and the rattles and squeaks of the saloon body. As we approached the junction where the road to Mondello forked off to avoid the military zone I leaned towards him and said :

'Can't we go straight on ?'

'No, it's forbidden.' He glanced quickly at me. 'Why do you want to go that way ?'

'For two reasons. First of all because it will be cooler. And secondly just because it is forbidden. It's always fun to do something which nobody else has done.'

45

He smiled without speaking. But when we came to the fork he lifted his foot from the accelerator.

'We're bound to be stopped,' he objected.

'I bet we won't be. You've got such an air of authority. Besides nobody would expect you to be in the military zone unless you had a pass.'

He turned the steering wheel away from the road to Mondello and drove into the forbidden zone. There was nothing to stop us. No barrier, no gate, no sentry, nothing but the big square notice-board.

The road was unmetalled and the lieutenant drove slowly so that the heavy yellow dust should not billow up and choke us – we had to keep the windows open, because it was so hot.

There were no trees and the sun beat down on the sand and shrivelled grass, even the sea glittered hotly. My companion must have thought me mad to suggest that it would be cooler here than on the shady inland road.

I soon saw why this was a forbidden zone. Huge guns pointed threateningly out to sea, concrete pillboxes were sunk into the sand, there were enormous rolls of barbed wire. I had stumbled upon one of the most heavily defended strips of coastline in Europe.

It was a sight which any secret agent would dream of. But I was appalled by it. How could I, so unfamiliar with guns and military equipment, possibly describe what I was seeing. Here was an opportunity which anybody else in the Deuxième Bureau would have made inestimable use of. And it was slipping away from me, unregistered, for even if I could have understood what I was seeing how could I remember so much?

Only the camera could help me. And, travelling in a car with an Italian officer, how could I use it? I was in despair.

The sense of frustration mounted in me and to relieve the tension I started to hum, then to sing.

'What a lovely voice you've got. Do go on.'

'Oh I can't,' I said. 'I'm awfully shy about my singing. I can't bear anyone watching me.'

'Oh do,' he coaxed.

'All right, I tell you what I'll do. I'll climb into the back.' Before he could protest I had clambered across the seat.

'Can you see me in the mirror?' I enquired coyly.

'Unfortunately no.'

I began to sing an old Neapolitan folksong and drew the Leica from my bag. In that brilliant sunshine I could not go wrong. All I had to do was to close the aperture to its limit and set the shutter speed as fast as it would go. With the car moving so slowly the picture would be sharp and clear.

Click, click, click. And every time I clicked the shutter I hit a high note. In any case the noise of the car would almost certainly have drowned the sound of the camera but I was taking no chances. Not that sort of chance anyway. My only worry was that I would forget to wind on the film and so make a double exposure. Each picture would be precious – I would need all thirty-six.

I moved in time to the music, swinging the camera to the left, to the right, straight ahead, then twisting round and pointing it out of the back window. I was photographing everything I saw and seeing only what I photographed.

'Lucky this is a four-light body,' the lieutenant remarked as the road curled inland and we left the military zone.

'What does four-light mean?'

'This car. It's only got windows in each door. There's a big blank space behind the back ones. So nobody can see if there's anyone in the back.'

'But was there anybody outside? I didn't notice anybody.'

'I expect you were too busy singing. Actually there weren't many soldiers about. It's the hottest time of day. And they're an idle lot, these Sicilians,' added this Italian officer patronisingly.

I hardly listened to what he was saying. My mind was full of the thirty-six pictures I had taken, of guns, and gun emplacements, pillboxes, gun tractors. To me the yellow and green camouflage, so appropriate to that sunbaked shoreline made the guns look like huge dead snakes, stretched straight and stiff. But to the Deuxième Bureau the photographs would tell every single military detail of this key defence position.

My hardest task was to conceal my elation from my nice lieutenant. I was bursting with excitement and pride. How thrilled the Deuxième Bureau was going to be!

Mother was no better that evening and next morning she was a great deal worse. I, too, had diarrhoea and felt awful. We had no money for a doctor but the owner of the pensione insisted on calling one. He was used to these sudden infections caused by the heat and the flies.

'Drink lots of lemon juice and rice water. No other food. And when you're strong enough to walk up the stairs go on to the roof – it's enclosed, no one can see you, take all your clothes off and stand naked in the full sun. Two minutes the first day, three the second, and so on until you can stand a full ten minutes.'

'But I don't want to,' I wailed. 'The last thing I'm bothering about is a suntan.'

The doctor laughed. 'I'm not worrying about a suntan either. But if you do as I say you'll find the five minutes' agony will make you feel cool for the rest of the day.'

He was right. And, in addition, the diet he prescribed gave me a perfectly genuine reason for buying the lemons which I needed for the invisible ink to write to the Deuxième Bureau pleading for money. The letters were acknowledged, more chocolates arrived. But no money.

We had been in Palermo for nearly two months and even the kind pensione owner indicated that things could not go on like this indefinitely. We had arranged to borrow enough money from him for my mother to go back to Monte Carlo. She would then get the money from the Deuxième Bureau and herself post it to me, journeying to Ventimiglia just across the frontier, to get the Italian currency and post it in Italy. There really was no need for elaborate security measures and all this nonsense with boxes of chocolates. I was left behind as a sort of hostage.

Mummy completed her mission but the money, when it arrived in an envelope in the ordinary way, was only just enough to pay our bill and my fare. Nothing over to get my rings out of pawn.

I booked my tickets the following day and went with my nice lieutenant for a last swim at Mondello – but this time by the detour.

'No need to tempt Providence. It was fun to do what nobody else had done. But let's not try it twice,' he said. It was no hardship for me to agree.

To mark our last day together he bought me an extravagant lunch, all sorts of luscious things from the cold buffet which the Italians present so well. At the next table at this smart open-air restaurant on the beach sat a party of young Sicilians. In their clear self-confident voices they were discussing somebody called Mario.

'Yes, you know the German girl relented and he was let out.'

'Mario in gaol. Imagine!'

'And now he's worked up a sort of fantasy. Gone all romantic.'

A burst of laughter.

'But it's true. He really has. This girl is his saviour! He's sworn to make it his life's work to find her and marry her!'

I spooned up the last morsel of fruit salad and smiled at my escort.

'Shall we go?' I suggested.

The time, I felt, had come for me to leave Sicily.

Chapter 5

Returning to those two little rooms in that shabby hotel in Monte Carlo was a homecoming. And, what is more, the Deuxième Bureau gave me something very like a hero's welcome. To save time my mother had brought back from Sicily the film of the coastal defences so that it had already been processed and the pictures evaluated when I got back. Le Petit was tremendously excited as he explained the importance of these pictures – how they showed the calibre and grouping of the guns, the methods of camouflage, in fact they laid bare the system which the Italians had adopted for the defence of Sicily. The Italians had proved themselves to be outstanding construction engineers – their roads both at home and overseas were the envy of Europe – and my pictures gave many valuable clues to the methods which they would use to defend their country's exceptional length of coastline so long and narrow, so vulnerable to any enemy who could gain mastery of the Mediterranean.

With the back pay I received to replace the money which had not reached me by way of the chocolate boxes I was temporarily quite affluent. So, with the grinding restrictions of poverty removed, we were at last able to treat ourselves to a few luxuries, and she took delight in rising above the cramped and primitive conditions to produce bedroom banquets from the little gas ring.

I fully expected to be sent back to Sicily, and although I did not want to go back at least I would be able to get my few trinkets out of pawn. However, for the time being I pushed aside all thoughts of work and gave myself up to relaxation. The physical strain of all that trudging round the harbours of Palermo and Catania in the shrivelling heat had brought me to the edge of exhaustion, no less than the mental strain of being permanently on the alert. Yet I had begun to develop some of the requisites of a secret agent – the heightened perception, the awareness of what went on all round me. I was learning, too, to rely on my intuition to warn me of danger on the one hand and of opportunities on the other. I was like a dog which walks stiff-legged and with ears pricked towards a strange animal, ready to fight or flee on the instant.

But I was young and strong and in a few days I was ready for the next mission, even impatient for it, although I was happy enjoying every moment of my short holiday. After the Sicilian cauldron Monte Carlo in July seemed quite cool.

When Le Petit telephoned to arrange a meeting – this time in a bistro in Nice – I set off eagerly to learn what the mission would be.

He did not tell me at once. First he congratulated me again on my photographs of the Sicilian coast – the technical skill, the initiative I had displayed, the audacity. He flattered me extravagantly and I lapped it all up. When he had got me purring like a cat he told me what my mission would be.

'The Italian Navy has two battleships being reconstructed, the *Duilio* and the *Giulio Cesare*. It's obvious that no country would willingly go to war until its fleet was as strong as possible. So it's a fairly safe bet that Italy won't attack us before those battleships are ready. Your mission is to find out when that will be.'

I could see that this was going to be a mission of the utmost importance – and also of the utmost danger. I was at the same time thrilled and appalled. Thrilled that I had been chosen, appalled at the difficulties.

'Speed is vital,' Le Petit went on. 'If you failed, there wouldn't be time for any other agent to pick it up.'

It took me a few moments to digest this information and Le Petit mistook my silence for hesitation.

'You have proved yourself,' he urged. 'Only you can do it.' He knew exactly how to coax me. But it was not necessary. I had already accepted the challenge.

He told me exactly what was required of me. I must photograph the ships at regular weekly intervals so that the experts would be able to assess the progress of the construction and calculate when it would be finished. He stressed that this was the whole purpose of my mission. I must concentrate entirely on the weekly photography and nothing else.

This very precise briefing was quite different from the previous casual 'find out anything you can' type of order. This emphasized the importance of the mission but it also removed any chance of picking up something on the side. It would be total success or total failure.

'And where are these ships?' I asked.

Le Petit looked embarrassed. He offered me a cigarette and lighted it for me before he replied quietly, in a voice very different from his usual forthright tones.

'We don't know.'

Even though I am wildly optimistic and tend to let my enthusiasm run away with me I could not take this seriously. I had visions of myself walking hundreds and hundreds of miles in and out of every port in Italy for years and years and years. The war would begin, finish, and be forgotten and still I would be wandering in and out of harbours, an old woman hobbling along on a couple of sticks.

'Yes I know,' said Le Petit sympathetically. 'It sounds impossible. But then it would have sounded impossible if we'd asked you to photograph the forbidden military zone outside Palermo, or the gunpark at the barracks. And yet you did both those things.'

'At least I knew where those places were. I didn't have to find them. But never mind,' I said impatiently. 'Let's go on, where do I start?'

'Up to you.'

I decided to begin with Genoa, simply because it was the nearest naval dockyard. Suddenly I saw a way of ensuring at least partial success for the expedition, even though it would have no effect on the mission itself. I would send my mother to Savona where she could make notes of the shipping in the harbour and come to Genoa, quite near by, to tell me. It would not be difficult for her because Savona harbour was so small. Genoa, in contrast, is one of the biggest harbours in the world, and no single person could hope to observe all the shipping movements in it.

Le Petit readily agreed to my suggestion. He was thankful to be able to. He was uncomfortably aware that the mission he had given me was not one which anybody could reasonably be asked to undertake.

Try as I might I could work up no enthusiasm for this mission. I considered that the chances of finding the *Duilio* and the *Giulio Cesare* were infinitesimal. The search would be futile and dangerous. Previously I had been given plenty of scope and encouraged to use my own initiative but now I had been left to carry out orders in which I did not believe. It is not in my character blindly to accept instructions which do not seem to me to make sense.

However, it is also not in my character to shirk or skimp a duty and, as the mission had been given to me, I must do my best to make a success of it.

If anything I was even less enthusiastic when I reached Genoa. I had never been there before and although I knew it had a very large harbour I had not visualized how enormous it would be. I estimated that walking quickly along the seafront would take at least two and a half hours.

I booked in at a modest little hotel – I had left Mummy on the way – and set to work. But it seemed even more hopeless than I had expected. What I had entirely left out of my calculations was that some of the ships would be anchored so far out that their names could not be read from the shore. I would have needed a motor boat to get to them. Also, of course, I did not know where in this whole vast area of shipping to find the naval dockyard. And naturally I could not ask.

It was risky enough to ask where the individual ships were, but there was nothing else for it. So every time I saw a seaman I asked the same questions. 'Can you tell me where the *Duilio* is?' and received the same answer. 'No idea.' 'Then can you tell me where the *Giulio Cesare* is?' 'No idea.'

I wandered round that vast harbour for a week, every day covering a different part of it. It would have been hard enough to locate a ship which I knew to be there. But there was very little reason to suppose that the ones I was looking for were in Genoa at all. My questions became more and more casual. I had lost all interest in my mission which was getting thoroughly on my nerves.

'Can you tell me where the *Duilio* is?' I mumbled, hardly looking at the man while I waited for the answer 'No idea.' Then I would shuffle on to the next.

'Can you tell me where the *Duilio* is?'

'Yes, she's over there.'

It was such a shock that I had to ask him to repeat it. 'Yes, over there. About half an hour's walk in that direction.'

'And can you tell me where the *Giulio Cesare* is?'

'That I can't tell you. Sorry.' He smiled and hurried on.

I was not elated. I was not even relieved. I simply did not believe it. 'Over there' did not look in the least like a naval dockyard. All the ships – and there seemed to be thousands of them – had funnels of different colours – black and white funnels, orange funnels, red funnels, blue funnels. But not one of these ships was wearing warpaint.

All the same my informant was right. 'Over there' I did find the *Duilio*. It was a freighter bound for South Africa.

I was not disappointed. I had not expected to find the battleship.

What was important was that there were two *Duilios*. At least from now on I would not be taking an appalling risk every time I uttered the name. If somebody became suspicious I could always pretend that it was the cargo ship I was asking about.

A secret agent engaged on a mission always looks for points like this, points which can be relied on to confuse the issue if it comes to a showdown. The coincidence of two ships bearing the same name was my safety belt. It might never be needed but it was a comfort to know it was there.

And in the next three weeks I needed all the comfort I could get. Every day was the same. Ships, ships, ships. I knew I would never find the only two ships in the world which held the slightest interest for me. On and on I went, trudging round this great bewildering harbour for hours and hours every day, and like a dull throb in my brain was the thought that this was the end of my career. I had been repeating the names of those two ships in time with my steps – *Duilio, Duilio, Giulio Cesare* – until I thought I should go mad. But now my marching song took on a mocking tone – 'Edita couldn't find them. Edita couldn't find them.'

I had started out with a 'sensible' pair of shoes and these shoes seemed to reflect my own weariness. They grew old and shabby in those three weeks. I never polished, never even wiped them. They lost their shape and spread out so that it looked as if I had feet like a duck. They were so ugly. I hated those shoes with a sullen hatred.

The only relief to the gloom of those three weeks was when my mother came over from Savona to give me the names of the ships in the harbour there. It was something to be able to send this information to the Deuxième Bureau. Not much, but something. Otherwise for all they knew I might have been dead. And for all *I* knew they might have wanted me to be dead. Perhaps they regarded me as expendable – an agent of so little value that she could be thrown away on a completely hopeless mission.

I emphasized, in my talks with Mummy, how important the information she was collecting would be. Other agents in other ports would report the names of the ships in their harbours and so the progress and route of each of the ships she had seen in Savona would be plotted. And from this collected information the Intelligence Service would be able to work out all sorts of things – which, added to other collected information, would indicate how Italy was planning to fight the coming war.

If Genoa had not been alive with uniforms, if the radio had not been blaring truculence, if all the talk in the cafés had not been of war, war, war, Genoa railway station itself would have been enough to show that war was imminent. With giant liners plying to all corners of the earth Genoa was a favourite embarkation place for passengers from the whole of Europe and consequently the railway station was permanently thronged with people anxious to know the latest news – what had happened while they had been journeying? The station bookstall displayed newspapers in many languages and I used to read the headlines while I was waiting to meet Mummy's train. Everybody was making speeches. Hitler a menacing one, Mussolini a bombastic one, Chamberlain a conciliatory one, Daladier an enigmatic one. And above the hiss and rumble of the trains I could hear a band playing martial tunes and a black-shirted procession chanting their battlesong – 'Corsica, Tunis, Nice'. Then, as now, people thought that if they shouted loudly enough they would get what they wanted. And then, as now, sometimes they were right.

I could not shout. I could only walk. With every leaden step I was wasting a little more of the precious time left to me, plodding round the maze of quays and jetties in Genoa while men were working feverishly to complete those two great battleships so that Italy could go to war confident in the might of her navy. Dulled with despair, I had given up looking at ships. I just followed those old shoes, dirty and full of dust.

It was hot and when I reached the edge of one quay it was too much of an effort to decide whether to turn left or right. I slumped down on the wall and dangled my legs over the side.

'What is a little girl doing up there?' I looked down and saw a rowing boat with a man in a blue jersey regarding me. He had a grey beard and there were lines of laughter round his eyes.

'Resting my feet. I'm tired. So tired.' And then it came out, the inevitable question in all its hideous familiarity.

'Can you tell me where the *Duilio* is?' But by now I had embroidered it a little, rather as one moves round the furniture in a room one dislikes in order to break the sickening monotony. 'You see, that's my fiancé's ship and I can't find it.'

The old boatman laughed.

'There.' He pointed. 'Just there, in front of you.'

I looked in blank disbelief. It was something, a big something, sticking several feet out of the water. It was red. I had seen it – I could not help seeing it. It was hardly farther away than my great ugly shoes. But I had not recognized it for what it was – the hull of a ship under construction.

'*That* thing?' I asked incredulously. 'The *Duilio*?'

The old boatman laughed again. 'Yes, that's the *Duilio* right enough. But your fiancé can't be serving on her.'

'Then I suppose I've got it wrong. I thought he was on the *Duilio* while he was waiting for the *Giulio Cesare* to be finished. But if the *Giulio Cesare* is anything like the *Duilio* it's going to be a long time.'

'Oh no. The *Giulio Cesare* is nearly finished. A fine ship. Would you like to see her?'

'I'd love to. How can I get there?'

'You can't. At least not without going out of the dockyard by the side entrance – the way you came in. Then you'd have to walk right round to the main entrance.'

So I was in the naval dockyard.

'Even then you wouldn't be able to get near her. She's anchored six hundred metres out.'

I was dismayed. Maddening if this wonderful find turned out to be too far away for me to photograph.

'I could row you round her if you like,' the boatman added.

I clambered down into his boat in a dream. I was dazed by the turn of fortune. It was so unbelievable, so marvellous. My only worry was whether I would be able to take photographs of the *Giulio Cesare*. The *Duilio* presented no problem. The enormous slab of nothing, that lifeless expanse of red iron – I could photograph that all right. Impossible to imagine that great ugly lump turning into anything as fine as a battleship with its sleek lines, its frowning turrets and its air of menacing power. Now it lay there like some forgotten hulk. There was no human being in sight.

As I began to take the photographs – eighteen here, eighteen for the *Guilio Cesare* – I looked at my watch so that I could be sure of being here next week at exactly the same time. Twenty minutes to one. No wonder there were no shadows. No wonder, too, there were no workmen. They would all be at lunch.

The old man rowed slowly and it was easy for me to hold the camera steady.

'I'm mad about photography,' I explained. 'And the view of the mountains behind the city is magnificent.' It was. But not nearly as magnificent for me as the view of that shapeless red object which would one day be the *Duilio*.

The boatman had been right about the *Giulio Cesare*. Already it was a ship, even I could see that, gleaming with white paint.

My fingers tingled with excitement as I clicked the shutter and wound on the film. After all the weeks of frustration it was a supreme satisfaction. Not like the excitement I had felt when I was taking those photographs from the back of the car in the military zone on the way to Mondello. That had been thrilling but it was the result of an impulsive decision instantly put into effect. This was the result of weeks of work, walking and worry. It was a fulfilment, the most lavish possible reward. Excited though I was, I could appreciate it in an almost detached way.

'All right if I drop you here, miss? I usually stay over this side to ferry the men back to their ships in the afternoon.'

'But I shall get lost,' I protested. I had blundered into this naval dockyard which ought to have been one of the best guarded places in Europe. But it was too much to expect that I would be able to blunder out again a different way.

'I'll take you, don't fret. I've got a way of my own – don't fancy showing a pass at the gate every time.'

He led me over the rusty railway lines, tripping over coils of rope and huge girders lying haphazardly about. Then he stopped and pointed. 'That street leads right into the middle of Genoa.'

So I was out of the dockyard and only the old man knew I had been inside it.

'I *did* enjoy that,' I told him as I paid him. 'Could you take me again next week?'

'Any time you like, miss.'

I arranged to meet him at the same time, at the same place.

Even my ugly shoes became young and beautiful as I danced my way back to the hotel.

I bought a ball of wool and stuffed the film into it. Then I wrapped it up and sent it to one of the addresses in Italy which the Deuxième Bureau had given me. From there a carrier would smuggle it across the Alps into France. I wrote – lemon juice again – and told the Bureau what I had done.

The only thing which worried me was how I was going to get into the dockyard the following week. I must repeat exactly what I had done – and hope for the best. But I still could not understand how I had managed it this time without being challenged. Then suddenly I realized. It had been about midday – five minutes to twelve or perhaps five past. Twelve o'clock would be the time for the sentries to change. Obviously they did not overlap – perhaps their guardroom was some distance away and they timed their tour of duty from guardroom door to guardroom door, instead of spending the full two hours or whatever it was at the actual post.

Satisfied on this point, I had nothing to do but amuse myself until the next week. My mother came over from Savona. She was not particularly surprised that I had found the ships. She had expected all along that I would. She, who was such a shrewd judge of character that she had become the best woman poker player I had ever met, had in spite of all her intelligence an absolutely unlimited confidence in my abilities. Not, perhaps, in my intellectual capacity but in my ability to succeed. She took it for granted that if I set out to do something I would achieve my objective.

We spent some happy afternoons exploring Genoa and one day

we went to see its famous cemetery; it is unique, for unlike any other, it is entirely beautiful. For centuries the Italian genius for carving marble has been employed in fashioning elaborate family tombs, each one a work of art worthy of a place in a museum. And the setting is superb.

Mummy, looking down at the long expanse of Genoa, squeezed on to a narrow ledge between the soaring mountains and the sparkling sea, murmured, 'It's a perfect place. So peaceful. So beautiful. This is where I'd like to be buried.'

She could not spend every afternoon with me, but I had made friends with a girl who was staying in the same hotel, and we used to go about together, so I was not lonely. Her name was Rosalia and she came from Turin. Only nineteen, she was young for her age, very pretty and beautifully dressed. When I complimented her on her clothes she let me into a secret. Her boyfriend gave them to her – a naughty thing in 1939.

What a relief it was that I would not have to traipse all round Italy searching for those two ships in every naval dockyard!

At last the week was up. I did exactly the same as last time. Same route, same time – and, of course, same shoes. They had become magic shoes, a sort of talisman. Nobody stopped me, nobody took any notice of me. The old boatman was waiting there, proud to show me round his beloved harbour once again, flattered that I had come back, as I promised.

'But of course I came,' I told him. 'It's such fun and so beautiful. In fact I'll try and come next week too.'

Perhaps I did not have quite the same feeling of elation, but still I enjoyed taking the photographs, I enjoyed the breeze coming off the sea. I did not think about the dangers or the difficulties. I knew I had to get into the dockyard, take the photographs and get out again. That was all. Everything else was irrelevant.

On every mission I adopted the same attitude of mind. It was a thread running through them all. I just got on with it, and did not allow myself to think. If anybody had stopped me and asked me what I was doing I would have given the first answer which came into my head. Whatever it was it would sound more natural – and therefore more innocent – than anything, however clever, which I might have prepared in advance. To think of what might or might not happen would have undermined my confidence and doubts would have niggled away at me like a canker. The mental state I deliberately created was like that of a sleep-walker. I did everything in a kind of dream, determined not to wake up until the mission was over. If sleep-walkers are suddenly awakened they fall down.

And so my shoes carried me into the dockyard, rested while I sat in the boat taking photographs, and carried me out again.

Just as on the previous occasion, I concealed the film in a ball of wool where no probing fingers would feel it through the wrapping and sent it off. This time it went to a different place, for although the same carrier would smuggle it from Italy to France, he would collect it from another address so that no two similar parcels should pass through the same postal channels. Again I notified the Deuxième Bureau.

The days while waiting for my next trip were boring. I went to the cinema with Rosalia, I rode on a tram, clanking from one end of Genoa to the other – well over ten miles it must have been – anything to pass the time.

Then came the day for the third visit to the dockyard. I walked, perhaps less steadily, less sure of myself, but I walked. I knew I had to.

I had loved the first time. I had enjoyed the second time. The third time was a burden. There was no joy in it.

When it was over I turned to the old boatman.

'I had hoped to bring a friend – a girl who is staying in my hotel. But she couldn't come today. So as not to disappoint her I shall have to come one more time.'

Even he, simple man though he was, might begin to wonder why I wanted to make four identical trips round the harbour. Worse, he might mention the matter casually to someone with a mind more suspicious than his own. Rosalia's presence would provide the perfect excuse for the final occasion.

When the third visit was over I felt the lifting of a great weight from my heart. Only one to go.

The first four days of the week were not boring at all, I dined with Mummy, Rosalia and I went sightseeing, it was a holiday.

Then a letter arrived from the Deuxième Bureau. They had received my three letters but no films.

It was a bald statement of fact. No clues as to what they

thought might have happened. No orders telling me what to do next.

My first reaction was one of dismay. Something terrible must have happened. Either the carrier had been caught or he had been a traitor and not taken the films. Whatever it was the result was clear. All my work had been wasted. The Deuxième Bureau had not got the information which they had been awaiting so anxiously. My part of the mission had been a tremendous achievement but the mission as a whole was a total failure. I might just as well have stayed in Monte Carlo.

I was so taken up with the bitterness of the disappointment that I did not immediately perceive the perils of the situation. Whether the carrier had been caught or whether he had betrayed us one thing was certain : by now my films would be in the hands of the Italian authorities.

There could be no mistaking the significance of the photographs. A film concealed in a ball of wool would arouse suspicions in any case. But in a country on the verge of going to war, with security precautions at a feverish height, these pictures of their new and secret battleship would instantly spark off the greatest alarm. And the greatest retribution.

I telephoned my mother and told her to return to Monte Carlo immediately.

Then I sat down to consider my own position. That the films could be traced to me there was no doubt. Inevitably the old boatman's head would appear in some of the pictures – I remembered that once or twice he had bent forward on his oars just at the moment when I was clicking the shutter.

I could flee. Or I could stay two more days and take the final film. If I fled it was likely that I would be arrested at the frontier. If I stayed and managed to take the final film there was just a chance that something could be saved from the ruin of the mission. If I could smuggle the film out at least the Deuxième Bureau would have one set of pictures. I decided to stay.

I was not arrested in the hotel. I had considered it a possibility but the fact that it had not happened was little relief for me. Why should they arrest me at the hotel when they could catch me red-handed as I stepped into the boat ?

I made sure that Rosalia was ready in plenty of time. My

success on the last two occasions had been due to my strict adherence to the timetable set by the first.

So convinced was I that I would be arrested as I stepped into the boat that it was more of an anti-climax than a relief when I was not. The old man greeted me warmly and Rosalia uttered a little cry of delight, overjoyed at the prospect of a trip round the harbour. She was still only a child in spite of the veneer of sophistication she assumed when talking of her boy-friend.

The great inert bulk of the *Duilio* loomed above us, expressionless as the Sphinx. As the old man pulled away from the quay I took the Leica from my bag and began to photograph.

'Oh do take one of me !'

'Sit still, then, and don't rock the boat.'

I took care that Rosalia's eager smiling face should not obstruct the important details of the photographs. From habit I took all eighteen of them from the same angles as I had before, even though the first three films were lost.

I rested the camera on my lap, behind my bag, as I always did. This was a period of inaction. The twenty minutes it took to cross the harbour far enough for the *Giulio Cesare* to come within range of my lens.

I could no longer brush my thoughts aside. I had steeled myself to enter the dockyard, steeled myself to face arrest when I reached the boat. Nothing had happened. But, with the passing of the danger, the tension did not slowly relax. It suddenly snapped.

The reaction took the form of extreme fear. I sat like a stone, unable to move.

Rosalia never stopped talking but I had no idea what she was saying. I was desperately battling with myself, summoning up all my reserves of courage. Only eighteen more photographs to take. Oh, if only it could be over.

How slowly the boatman rowed !

Now the *Giulio Cesare* was lying there waiting for me. All I had to do was to lift the Leica and start. I could not.

'Go *on* !' I told myself. 'Lift that viewfinder to your eye and get going. *Go on.*'

I could not.

Whoo, whoo, whoo.

The rising and falling wail of a police siren dragged the blood from my heart with each declining note.

I saw the boatman's mouth open. Rosalia stopped chattering in mid-sentence and her eyes widened with terror. Scudding across the waves towards us was a police launch, its slim prow pointed like a dagger at my breast.

The camera still lay on my lap, my bag across it. There was just time to slip it over the side, to sink with its mute accusation to the kindly depths of the harbour. I took the Leica in my hand.

Then I paused. With the camera would go the last hope of preserving any shred of success for my mission. I let the Leica slip back on to my lap.

The flurry of foam was almost upon us. Then the launch swooped round and drew up alongside, our little boat rocking on the angry waves it churned up.

Black menacing figures glared down at us.

'What the hell do you think you're doing? Who are you? Where do you come from?'

The barrage of questions beat into my brain. I was paralysed. I could not speak. I could not think. I was suspended in a nightmare.

Rosalia began to howl.

'We were only having a trip round the harbour. We weren't doing anything wrong. Oh why are you being so horrid?' She sobbed and choked.

'Where did you come from?'

'From Torino. And I wish I'd never left home. I was having such a lovely time here in Genoa. And now you've come along and ruined it all.'

In all her short spoilt life nobody had ever shouted at Rosalia before. 'Aaaah,' she howled.

'And where did *you* come from?' The question was shot at me.

'Also from Torino.' The lie was not incriminating. One of the ways of entering Italy from France is via Turin.

The senior policeman now turned his attention to the boatman.

The old man blubbered incoherently, scared out of what wits he had.

Rosalia redoubled her shrieks.

'Shut up,' yelled the policeman. She howled louder, the

boat shaking to her sobs. She was so obviously terrified, so obviously innocent. The policeman addressed the boatman again. He had to raise his voice to make himself heard above Rosalia's yells.

'Get these bloody women out of here.'

As the old man fumbled for his oars the launch sped away across the harbour.

The wail of the siren died away. The waves of the launch's wake quietened to a ripple. Except for the creak of the rowlocks and an occasional hiccup from Rosalia there was silence in our little boat.

I found that I had the use of my hands again. I lifted the Leica from my lap and took eighteen photographs of the *Giulio Cesare*.

Chapter 6

August 1939

Genoa station was almost deserted. In the seven weeks in which I had been in the city the war had quickened the pace of its approach. At first, when I went to the station to meet Mummy's train from Savona, it had been thronged with tourists hastening home to seek shelter from the coming storm. Now the holidays were over and Europe was holding its breath.

I settled myself in the corner of a second class compartment. I felt worn out after the anxiety of the past few days culminating in the horrible events of the afternoon and I was not willing to sit on the hard benches of the third class for four and a half hours in order to save the difference in the fare.

Mussolini, they used to say, even made the Italian trains run on time. I felt deeply grateful to him as, precisely at the advertised minute, we slid out of Genoa station. I was not surprised that I had the compartment to myself. The Italians were not travelling much. The lira was weak, the franc was strong, and people had been trying to smuggle money out. But it was no longer worth doing. The Customs searches were extremely thorough and the penalties severe. I knew that I must hide my precious film. The Leica did not matter – any tourist might have one. I had intended to conceal the film in the lavatory but as I was alone there was no need to go out of my compartment.

The windows of the carriage had curtains made of some stiff brown material and they were drawn back and held in position by looped leather straps. Before we reached the frontier I placed the film in one of these loops where it lay snugly out of sight. The curtains were grimy from the smuts of the coal-burning locomotive and I hated the thought of my beautiful film getting dirty. It had become the greatest treasure in the world.

With the film hidden in the curtain I felt safe for the first time in days. If by some mischance it should be discovered I would strenuously deny that it had anything to do with me. I had temporarily forgotten that Rosalia's smiling face appeared on several of the *Duilio* photographs so that the film could be traced to me with hardly any trouble at all.

I watched for a few minutes to make sure that the jolting of the train did not dislodge the film, but the stiffness of the material held it secure as it nestled in the pleats behind the leather strap. A few minutes before we reached the frontier the door opened and two Customs officers entered the compartment. They were polite and friendly as they searched first my suitcase and then my bag. The search was very thorough. These men were experienced, and if I had been carrying gold or diamonds in my luggage they certainly would have found them.

The train drew to a halt at Ventimiglia and when they had satisfied themselves that my suitcase contained no secret hiding places they thanked me, smiled and withdrew.

The whistle blew, there was a slamming of doors and a shuddering of wheels, the train jerked away from the platform. As soon as it gathered speed I jumped up and retrieved my precious film. I could not bear to be parted from it for a second longer than was necessary. It was dusty from its enforced stay behind the curtain and I carefully removed the smuts with my glove. Then I put it back in my bag. I rested my head against the cushions. The ordeal was over. With the rhythm of the wheels beating out a little tune of triumph, my treasure and I were speeding to freedom. At last I could relax.

Then the door of the compartment opened and the Customs officers reappeared. This time they had a woman with them.

As the train had been running into Ventimiglia I had made a conscious effort to control my anxiety. I had known that the Customs were coming, that their search would be thorough, and I had prepared myself. The shock of their return found me defenceless. I had no time to pull myself together.

The Customs officers were still friendly and pleasant. The woman, they explained, would search me.

'Don't bother to go through her suitcase and her bag. We've

done them,' one of them told her.

When I heard those words I nearly fainted, so great was the relief. But it was immediately succeeded by a terrible thought. Would she take any notice? Or would she search my bag herself? She might do it out of curiosity — one woman wanting to know what another was in the habit of carrying about with her, what lipstick she used. Or she might resent being given orders by a man, and search the bag to show her independence. I wished fervently that I had left the film safely hidden behind the curtain.

The rhythm of the wheels changed. We must be slowing down for the approach to Menton, I thought.

I slipped out of my dress and the woman glanced out of the window.

'We'll be in the station in a minute and we don't want anybody looking in,' she remarked. She reached across and undid the leather straps so that the curtains fell across the window.

I forced myself to relax my muscles as she ran her fingers expertly over the thin underclothes. In no account whatever must I show the slightest anxiety. Outwardly calm, inside I was frantic with fear, with worry, with relief.

'You can put your dress on now.'

I thought she would go. I thought it was over. But no. She stayed. I had my dress on. Perhaps she was waiting for me to open my bag and take out a comb. The tension was unbearable. In another second something would snap.

'Thank you. Good day,' she said and slid open the door.

'Good day to you.' It took me all my willpower to produce a smile.

Wonderful news was waiting for me in Monte Carlo. The first three films had arrived after all. I never discovered what had caused the delay. Le Petit did not tell me and I had learned not to ask questions.

He was tremendously excited. Apparently the photographs showed far more detail of the *Duilio* and the *Giulio Cesare* than anyone had hoped for. Not only had the experts been able to forecast the dates of completion of the two battleships but the pictures were clear enough for them to tell the specifications of armour and armament.

It was a triumph. For me, for Le Petit, for the Deuxième Bureau.

Then I gave him the fourth film.

He made me tell him exactly what had happened in the harbour, and when I described hiding the film in the curtain in the train he was appalled. At first he was furious with me for having taken such risks. Then suddenly he hugged me. The risks had been great but the results justified them.

He hurried off to have the film processed. Le Petit was a completely single-minded man, utterly dedicated to the cause he served. It gave him deep satisfaction that his protegé had made such an important contribution and he regarded me with a proprietorial air. I think he thought of himself as a sort of animal trainer, proud of a dog which could walk on its hind legs.

That afternoon he took me to see the *Commissaire de Police* in Beausoleil. Le Petit explained that normally the Deuxième Bureau and the police were antagonistic towards one another. The police considered the agents to be irresponsible amateurs, meddling in matters which would be better left to the professionals. The Bureau regarded the police as unimaginative, slow, and bound with red tape. The police envied the freedom of the Deuxième Bureau. The Deuxième Bureau envied the scope of the powers of the police. The members of the two organizations regarded each other with mutual suspicion, distrust, and contempt. The fact that they were both engaged on aspects of national security gave an extra vindictiveness to their hostility, making it something of a family feud.

But there were exceptions. And Seraphin Ailhaud, *Commissaire de Police* at Beausoleil was one of them. This middle-aged bachelor was more like a bank manager than a policeman. Formal to the point of fussiness, he had a decisive mind and an independent spirit. Le Petit told me that if ever I was in trouble Ailhaud would instantly help. I found this easy to believe.

A few days later I was summoned to Nice. Not, this time, to the Hotel Alsace-Lorraine, but to an office block at 13, rue Grimaldi, a quiet turning off the rue de France. I climbed, as instructed, to the fourth floor and knocked on the appointed door.

It was not Le Petit who opened in answer to my knock but

the older man with the prominent nose, whom I had nick-named 'The Admiral'.

He greeted me warmly. If I had previously had any doubts as to whether he was head of our section I had them no longer. His air of authority was indisputable. But he was in a gentle mood.

My achievements, he said, had been remarkable. Sicily had shown that I had initiative and my exploits in Genoa had proved conclusively that I had courage as well as brains.

The little room was almost as characterless and functional as the one in which I had received my training. But as I listened blissfully to The Admiral's praise it became a ballroom in a fairy palace. And I was a fairy princess in silver shoes.

The Admiral was cataloguing my successes – emphasizing how each had shown that I was capable of acting on my own initiative, as opportunity offered, improving upon the orders I had been given.

So well had I done, he told me, that our section had received a letter from the head of the French Navy, Admiral Darlan, commending us for the valuable information obtained in Genoa.

'Admiral Darlan indicates that the agent who did this exceptionally fine work should be recommended for a high decoration,' The Admiral told me. Then, smiling, he added, 'Admiral Darlan doesn't know the sex of the agent.'

He went on to explain that, alas, he could not recommend me for the award which I unquestionably deserved. The announcement of such an award to a woman would attract tremendous publicity – and publicity was something he could not risk.

'You told me you were going to be our star. And now you are.'

It was heady stuff. But when I am profoundly moved, as I was then, I conceal my feelings. I brushed it all aside, lightly, almost cheekily.

But there was more to come. As a compensation for not recommending me for the award which I merited he was going to make me a present. There was, it appeared, a fund from which regular agents could be paid sums for special purposes. I might like, he suggested, to take a flat. More comfortable than living in a hotel. He handed me an envelope.

Then, a few more graceful compliments, and he bowed me out.

As soon as I got out of the door I counted the notes. Ten thousand francs! Over three months' pay!

Mother, who acted as treasurer for our slender finances, was delighted and gave me a little lecture about regarding it as the foundation of a capital. But she insisted that I buy a lovely pink raincoat and she was as eager as I was to buy a few extra things – undreamed of luxuries like lobsters, shimmering silk stockings and one gorgeous meal (lobster again) at a smart restaurant instead of our scruffy bistro.

We were perfectly happy in our shabby little rooms. Even the huge sum of ten thousand francs was not enough to buy the lease of a flat and furnish it. Besides, Monte Carlo had already been evacuated once. When war – now agreed to be imminent – came, it would undoubtedly be evacuated again. So there was no point in taking a flat. Much better, Mummy urged, to invest the capital. How much was common sense and how much unselfishness I could not tell. For some time I had been worried about my constant crossings of the frontier with Italy. The Italian consul in Monte Carlo always gave me a visa without question. Anybody who lived in Monte Carlo was assumed to be rich and as far as he was concerned these frequent journeyings might have been an eccentricity in which I had the money to indulge. Besides, the consul was probably unpaid, doing the job solely for prestige, an amateur in all senses of the word. But the Fascist police and Customs officers were something else. I needed to be able to give some convincing reason if I were ever questioned as to why I was making all these trips.

I thought about it for a long time. Finally I came to the conclusion that the best thing would be a sort of double bluff. I would do something slightly shady which, if discovered, would serve to divert attention from my real and deadly crime. I would try my hand at a little gentle smuggling. But what should I smuggle?

Diamonds? Out of the question, with only the change from ten thousand francs. Gold? Certainly I could not afford enough to be convincing. Besides, I knew nothing whatever of the bullion market. Under interrogation I would soon betray the depths of my ignorance.

Suddenly I got it. Furs. On those interminable walks in Genoa, killing time with Rosalia, we had gawped into every shop window, pricing everything from tiaras to tomatoes. I had noticed that furs were substantially more expensive in Italy than in France, so furs it must be.

Monte Carlo was full of furriers. In the late summer they were hopefully preparing for the autumn and winter markets but they were realistic enough to trim their prices to the current economic climate. I found an Algerian in a back street, told him what I intended to do, and promised that if I was successful I would return to him. He sold me a Persian lamb coat and a silver fox fur – the height of prevailing fashion – at a price which I recognized as considerably below that obtaining in Italy.

Two days later Le Petit called me to Nice – Hotel Alsace-Lorraine as usual – to brief me for my next mission. The Deuxième Bureau knew that I had spent some time in Venice the previous year (it was there that I had met Giuseppe Castellano) and, as they had no resident agent there, they wanted me to go, with two objectives. Firstly I was to test the possibilities of setting up an espionage network and secondly – a forlorn hope this – to see whether it would be possible to photograph the island naval base of Marghera.

On the way to Venice I changed trains at Milan and took the opportunity of going to look at the cathedral. As I was walking back to the station I heard my name called. Bustling out of a café came a figure I had known well in the old days. He had been a great friend of my father, almost as great a friend as Eman Petera. But anyone less like the tall and stiff colonel than this round little man with shiny black hair and the name of Goldstein would be hard to imagine.

He took me into the café and we spent a happy half hour comparing experiences – his, like mine, no doubt carefully edited – since his abrupt departure from Vienna just before the Nazis marched in. At that time anybody with a name like Goldstein needed to have a strong talent for survival and he had a genius for it. He had equipped himself – quite legitimately – with a Turkish passport and was living in a suite at one of Milan's best hotels happily doing currency deals.

I was heartened by this encounter. If ever I ran out of money he would be delighted to help and I could always be sure of a welcome from him and his wife whenever I chanced to be in Milan.

On my previous visit to Venice I had stayed at the Lido but now I wanted to be right in the heart of the city so I walked into the first small hotel I came to as I left the Piazza San Marco. By lucky coincidence I chose well for the owner was a Czech, Josef Koci. He had lived in Italy for more than twenty years but was still firmly Czechoslovakian.

'What do you think of the way those dirty French and those dirty British let us down?' he enquired indignantly. 'They ought to have given that Hitler a punch on the nose.'

For all his militant talk I could not picture Koci himself giving anybody a punch on the nose. Years of the starchy foods which Czechs love had given him an impressive paunch and he was built for comfort not speed. He was frank about his political views. Fascism was good for Italy – look how Mussolini had pulled the country together – and many of the friends he had made ten or twenty years ago had become Fascists. They were his friends still. He himself had no desire to live anywhere other than Venice even though he had to admit that the narrow canal on which his hotel was situated did stink a trifle in hot weather.

There was nothing wrong with the Italians. The only trouble was this stupid Axis pact. How a man as wise and clever as Mussolini – a family man too – could go and get himself mixed up with a mountebank like that Hitler, Josef Koci could not conceive.

There was no need to sound him out cautiously. Hitler had gobbled up Czechoslovakia and it was the duty of every Czech to fight him to the death. I felt that Koci would fight in every way he could, short of actual fighting.

I told him I was making a small contribution. Koci bounced up and down on his round bottom and squeaked with excitement. How fortunate I was! He wished that he had such a chance. Was there, perhaps, some way he could help me? There was indeed.

In many ways Koci would make an ideal secret agent. He knew everybody and everybody knew him. Fascists talked quite freely in front of him, accepting him as one of themselves in spite of his atrocious accent. Any titbits of gossip that were going Koci was bound to hear.

Another factor in favour of enrolling him was that many

Germans stayed in his hotel, attracted by Mrs Koci's suet puddings. By coincidence it was called the Excelsior, but it was only a faint echo of the one in Palermo. A great advantage was that, being inexpensive, it was frequented more by junior officers than by senior ones who would be less likely to allow their tongues to become loosened in the bar. Against that, it was true that the older officers would know more. But in fact that was not very important. The armed forces of every nation had, by 1939, become so specialized that probably only very senior commanders knew the overall strategy. What an agent had to concentrate on was gathering details which might seem trivial in themselves but which made very great sense when added to others obtained from different sources. So the garrulous subalterns in Koci's bar might very well provide valuable information. It would, for instance, be possible to deduce from their conversation where their units were stationed.

Koci was bubbling with enthusiasm and full of ideas. Oh yes, many of the tradesmen who supplied his hotel also supplied the army camps – simple to find out from them when one regiment left and another arrived. And who better to tell him what ships were moving in and out of Marghera and Mestre than the men who fished the lagoon?

Most of these people would give the information unwittingly but a few of them could be asked to find out specific information. How much, Koci enquired, would be available for paying them?

This was a question I could not answer on my own. The Deuxième Bureau were not very good at paying their agents. They considered it an honour to work for them and people should not ask for money. They should be proud to serve for no reward.

I saw that I would have to return to France to acquaint the Deuxième Bureau with some of the facts of Venetian life. I stayed in Venice only long enough to photograph Marghera from a considerable distance and to sell the furs to a furrier in the next street. As I had thought, I was able to make a modest profit on them. This was very satisfactory. Not only did it provide an excellent reason for coming so often to Italy but it also would satisfy my mother-treasurer that I had made a sound investment.

I promised Koci that I would be back soon, and took a last look round Venice before leaving. It was sad to see how great were the changes since I had last been there under a year before. It was not unchanging Venice that had changed – it was the people. Now there were uniforms everywhere, flags waving, bands playing, radios blaring martial music.

I found it terribly sad that these people so civilized, so witty, so charming, should have been persuaded to ally themselves with the bestiality of Nazi Germany. But, I told myself, they would soon learn a sharp lesson. The might of France and Britain would very soon put paid to Hitler and all his hangers-on. The shock of defeat would bring the Italians to their senses.

On the telephone Le Petit sounded delighted that I had come back so soon.

'It can only be a matter of days before the war begins,' he said.

I met him at the Hotel Alsace-Lorraine and told him about Koci and the plans we had worked out. He promised that the vetting of Koci would start immediately.

'As soon as we know he's all right we'll send someone to Venice to give him his instructions.'

I was puzzled.

'But that'll be me, surely,' I said.

'You? Oh no. Your next mission is already fixed. You're to go back to Palermo.'

Chapter 7

September 1939

I stared at Le Petit in dismay. To be sent back to Palermo was the last thing I wanted or had expected. And, it was not to be for a few days only. The intention was that I should stay there for the duration of the war, a daunting prospect. Obviously it would be impossible during wartime to send agents to Sicily whenever they were needed. Therefore it was essential to have one resident there who could carry out orders transmitted from France.

Not that we thought that the war would last very long. I would, I told my mother, be home for Christmas. I gave her explicit instructions about storing my evening dresses and then, arrayed in my lovely new pink raincoat, I set off for Sicily. Mummy did not say much but there were tears in her eyes as she kissed me good-bye.

One good thing about it was that I would be able to get my rings out of pawn. Le Petit had assured me that this time there would be no trouble about money. Several other agents had complained that they had received boxes of chocolates with no money in them and it had since been discovered that the paymaster had taken the money to the local Casino hoping to increase it before he sent it on. I was interested to hear the reason for the non-arrival of my money but mortified to learn that the Deuxième Bureau had not believed me until other agents had made similar complaints.

'If you thought I could do something like that you ought to have dismissed me,' I said angrily. But Le Petit laughed and shook his head. 'Not likely. You had already become far too valuable to lose.'

By now my honour had been cleared and I was proudly marching off to war. That the war would start within hours there could be no doubt. The Nazis had invaded Poland, and

France and Great Britain would spring to arms immediately. It was an enormous relief that at last Hitler would get his retribution, swift and sure.

It was a wonderful time to be alive. The years of uncertainty were over. In a few months from now Europe would be purged of National Socialism for ever. My only regret was that I was going to be tucked away in the backwater of Palermo while all these exciting events would be taking place. How much more thrilling if I could have been in Monte Carlo with Mummy, exulting with her over the defeat of Hitler. Even though Monaco was so close to Italy I knew there would be no danger. The defences of the Alpes Maritimes were impregnable and the poor misguided Italians would never penetrate them, while in the north the gallant French Army would, of course, sally forth from the great fortress of the Maginot Line to crush the Germans.

My morale was very high. When the train pulled into Rome I jumped down before it had quite stopped, eager to hear the latest news.

The station was in an uproar. Wild rumours were seized upon, enlarged, passed on and forgotten as fresh, wilder rumours succeeded them. I felt that I was being tossed backwards and forwards on a sea of excited speculation.

It was some time before I was able to discover that France and Great Britain had declared war on Germany. Everybody was shouting, everybody was happy. Hitler would soon show those cheeky dogs where they got off. The morale of the Italians who milled round me on the platform was just as high as my own. And when would the train leave for Naples? Ah, who could say? Not for many hours, certainly. But why bother about Naples? Rome was the place to be, today of all days. At this moment – even at this very moment – Il Duce was speaking from his balcony. If I went at once I might still be in time to hear him. Hurry, hurry, hurry.

And so I found myself among the thousands thronging the wide Piazza Venezia. Thousands and thousands of patriotic Italians and one French spy.

And yet I did not feel myself to be on hostile territory, alone in the midst of a vast crowd of enemies. I really loved the Italians and I felt at home among them. But how could I allow myself to be sentimental? They had allied themselves with Hitler, an uneasy alliance with suspicion on both sides, but an alliance nevertheless. And for this they must be punished. I felt like a mother chastising naughty children. Beat them, certainly. But hate them? Never. The idea was absurd.

Italian is a deeply emotive language and in the mouth of a master it has great beauty. Mussolini was such a master, and the throb and flow of his cadences cast a spell upon that eager throng. I had the sensation of being at the hub of history.

'Our aircraft will darken the skies.'

The words, boastful, bombastic though they were, rolled majestically round that huge square, clear and strong like the notes of a gigantic organ. The applause rose up like a tidal wave, echoed again and again. He had the power of rousing the people he led to a crescendo of emotion.

'Our aircraft will darken the skies.'

I almost believed him myself. I almost *wanted* to believe him.

But Mussolini did not declare war.

Eventually I got to Naples. Chaos. No ferries to Sicily. No hope of any ferries to Sicily. No hope at all. Nothing.

I had not bargained for this. Nor, I suspected, had the Deuxième Bureau. They had intended to plant me in Sicily for the duration of the war and they had assumed that I would get there.

I felt inadequate and uncertain. Ought I to go somewhere else? If so, where? The Bureau had placed their agents, they would not want me duplicating somebody else. I had been given an address in Italy where I was supposed to send my reports which would then be taken over the mountains by a carrier. This had been foreseen because obviously the Franco-Italian frontier would be closed on the outbreak of war. The Deuxième Bureau did not expect me to return to France while the war lasted otherwise they would have made some provision for getting me across the frontier. They had not.

I myself had taken the precaution of getting a transit visa which would allow me to travel through – though not stay in – Switzerland. Everybody knew that the Swiss always remained neutral and if the worst came to the worst I could escape from

Italy over the Swiss frontier. It gave me a sense of security. But I hesitated to use it. My orders had been perfectly clear. Go to Palermo.

In my dilemma I decided to take the French consul into my confidence and ask his advice. I sought him out at his home and I was thankful that, after long thought, he advised me to return through Switzerland.

Easier said than done. Italy was not yet actually at war but everybody expected her to be shortly. Everybody wanted to get home. Everybody in Naples wanted to go to Rome. Everybody in Rome wanted to go to Naples. The chaos mounted.

Days later the train disgorged me in Lucerne. It was not my choice. The train simply stopped there so I had no choice. Just as well, for I was beyond making choices.

On the platform was a reception committee of nuns – two reception committees. I chose the Catholics. They took me in, not patronizingly, but willingly, joyfully, delighted to be of service. I was borne along on a wave of spiritual love.

With my transit visa I was not entitled to do more than pass through Switzerland. But the Mother Superior – compassion shone in her beautiful eyes – would have kept me for the whole war if necessary. Ten days was all I asked. In that time I expected an answer to the letter I wrote to the Deuxième Bureau asking for orders. None came.

It was tempting to linger in the atmosphere of that convent, so clean, so pure, and so happy. But I became restive. I was of the world and I must get back to it. There was work to be done.

So I emerged from this haven of security and squeezed myself into the corridor of a train bound for France. When we reached the frontier at Bellegarde we had to get out and go through the passport control. It took a very long time with so many people all desperate to return to their own country – the French shouting and gesticulating, the English sitting resignedly on their suitcases. I was impatient like the rest but I had no worries. My Czech passport was in order and I had a residential visa for Monaco.

'That's no good. When France declared war all visas like this were automatically cancelled. You'll have to get a new one.' The officer was curt.

'But I live in Monte Carlo, it's my home,' I protested. The

officer was adamant. I must, it appeared, get a new visa from the Monaco consul. It was annoying. Going into the town would cause a delay and I should probably miss the train.

'What's his address?' I asked.

'Don't know. Geneva somewhere.'

'*Geneva*! But I can't go all the way to Geneva. I haven't got the money for the fare. And I've only got a transit visa for Switzerland. I can't travel all over the country. I'd be arrested.'

'That's your problem,' he said unsympathetically. 'Next.'

I suppose it was the contrast with the kindness I had received at the hands of the nuns that made it seem so dreadful. But it was in any case a very serious problem. I paced up and down the platform wondering what to do.

'I heard your trouble. I was behind you in the queue. I would like to help, my child.'

I swung round and found myself looking into the smiling face of an old French lady. She opened her crocodile bag and took out a roll of notes. 'Please,' she said, holding them out to me.

'But I can't take them,' I exclaimed. 'I mean you don't know anything about me. And how will I ever get them back to you?'

'It doesn't matter. Some day somewhere you will find somebody who needs help. Do what you can for them.' She nodded, smiling, and turned away.

Her kindness brought me back to life, my self-confidence returned in a flood. I was a member of the Deuxième Bureau. How ridiculous that these petty officials should try to order me about when all I wanted to do was to go home!

I picked up my suitcase and hopped back on the train. I locked myself in the loo until it had started and when it was safely bowling through France I emerged. As I walked up the train looking for a seat I came to the carriage where the old lady was sitting. She beckoned me to wait and came out into the corridor to speak to me.

'The police have been looking for a woman in a pink raincoat. I'm afraid it must be you. Wouldn't it be better to give yourself up at the next station? I'm sure you haven't done anything very wrong.'

On reflection I realized that her advice was sound. Star of the Deuxième Bureau I might be but from any point of view my action had been high-handed. It would be best to apologize to the police, explain the circumstances, and close the incident. Accordingly, at the next station I alighted from the train and approached an *agent de police*.

Immediately there was uproar. Policemen came running from all directions, waving machine guns. The more I explained the more they ranted, the more they ranted the angrier I became. Without doubt I must be a spy! All the world knew that Czechoslovakia was part of Germany. It was clear that I was a German spy. What effrontery! What impertinence! To flout the law was bad enough but for the purposes of espionage! I must be guarded with extreme care. So grave was my offence that I must at once be returned to Bellegarde and there be charged.

A policeman was despatched to commandeer a locomotive and the rest of us filled in time by standing on the platform screaming at one another. They could not have made more fuss if they had caught Mata Hari herself.

Eventually the locomotive puffed importantly into the station and we all clambered aboard. I sat there, smouldering with fury, glaring defiantly at the unwavering machine guns.

All this had taken a long time and, it was three o'clock in the morning by the time we got to Bellegarde. I immediately demanded that the Commissaire de Police be summoned. They were shocked. More impertinence! To awaken such an important man at that hour! Unthinkable!

'Get the Commissaire,' I insisted. My rage had reached the point where my voice, though quivering slightly, became low and controlled. The contrast with the previous explosions of anger must have impressed them. They sent for the Commissaire.

'Kindly telephone your colleague Seraphin Ailhaud at Beausoleil,' I said, politely imperious, trying to make myself ten foot tall. 'I know that he will be at home asleep but you can find the number and wake him up.'

I do not know what passed between them but when the Commissaire returned he was smiling. The next train was not due for an hour and a half – and who knew, with a war on, whether it would be punctual – he told me. But even if it were, there would still be enough time for a delicious meal to be prepared and eaten. Happily one of his policemen was a superb chef, a veritable cordon bleu ...

The journey from Bellegarde to Monte Carlo took, incredibly, three days and two nights. Every few miles, it seemed, I had to change trains, or mine would be shunted into a siding to allow priority to a military train crammed with soldiers, laughing and waving, singing the Marseillaise. It ought to have been a grim and wearying experience but it was not. Everybody was elated and I was caught up in the war fever, the great wave of patriotism sweeping over a great country going to war for a just cause. Only two weeks before in Rome I had seen the Italian expression of the same sentiment. Try as I would to be an aloof observer I found myself beginning to share the excitement. But now I had no inhibitions. This was France, my France, the one country out of all the world which I had chosen to be my own. I could participate in the grand emotional patriotism, I could feel tremendous exhilaration and express it to the full. I shouted the words of the Marseillaise, those fine stirring words, until my lungs ached.

France, France, France. I would live for France. I would die for France.

I was drunk with excitement and fatigue when I burst into Mummy's bedroom at six o'clock in the morning. Oh! what joy, what hugging, what kissing. Then I fell asleep.

Later, much later, I telephoned the Deuxième Bureau. I need not have worried about my failure to get to Palermo. Le Petit was immensely relieved to know that I was safe. None of my letters had arrived, he had no idea what had happened to me or where I was. I must come and tell him all about it. Next day, at our usual rendezvous the Hotel Alsace-Lorraine. By that time he would have obtained fresh orders for me.

The orders turned out, when I met him, to be exactly what I would have chosen myself. I was to return immediately to Venice.

It was marvellous. No fear now of being stuck away for the whole war in a backwater like Sicily. Poor sad Sicily, good-bye! And if it meant that my few trinkets would be lost for ever in the pawnshop – well, never mind. I was off to Venice.

All previous plans had been based on the assumption that Italy would declare war simultaneously with Germany. Now that it was apparent that Mussolini was in no great hurry to plunge his country into war the Allies had a precious breathing space which must not be wasted. It was essential to redouble our efforts to find out all we could about the enemy and the potential enemy. My orders were clear. To recruit any agents I could, to gather every speck of information about shipping and troop movements – German ships were of course using the ports of neutral Italy – and to report on the attitude of the Italians towards the Germans and of the Germans towards the Italians.

Le Petit and I were young and very junior members of our organization and we were told only what was necessary for us to know. This did not in any way inhibit us from considering ourselves amateur strategists and we came to the conclusion that Mussolini had not only drawn back from the brink of war but that there was a glimmer of hope that he might split with Hitler altogether and turn to our side. In spite of the fact that Hitler had introduced a new horror and a new word – *blitzkrieg* – to Europe and that Poland was already dying beneath the tracks of Nazi tanks, we were confident that Hitler would never attack France. Only a madman would assault the Maginot Line and even Hitler was not mad enough for that.

The thought that a rift might develop between the partners of the Axis lent romance and excitement to my assignment. I was eager to start.

But there was a formidable obstacle.

The friendly Italian consul refused me a visa. He explained patiently and apologetically that Czechoslovakian passports were no longer valid and that anyway mine was out of date. I ought to have changed it months before for a German one.

Naturally, with France and Germany at war the last thing I wanted was a German passport even if I could have got one. I determined to go and see Commissaire Seraphin Ailhaud. I owed him a visit in any case, to apologize for disturbing him in the middle of the night and to thank him for his help.

Ailhaud greeted me warmly. Then I asked him to give me a French passport. He stared at me in horror.

'Madness!' he exclaimed. 'Madness! You won't get across the frontier. Passport control officers are trained to remember –

you will be recognized and they'll remember you had a Czech passport before.'

'Before I've always gone by train. This time I shall go by bus to Ventimiglia and get a train there. It'll be a different lot of passport control officers.'

'But when you get to Venice you are going back to the same hotel. The porter will remember you had a Czech passport last time.'

'Exactly. He will have all the particulars written down. And this time he'll just copy them out. He won't even ask to see the passport.'

It took all my powers of persuasion but once Ailhaud was convinced he did not hesitate. He procured a passport for me, filled in with precisely the same particulars as my old one. Even the photographs were similar because I had duplicates of the original ones. It was highly irregular, so highly irregular that he was risking his career, his job, his pension. But this dedicated man considered the risk worthwhile.

I took an early bus from Monte Carlo to Nice so that I could do some shopping before catching one to get me to Ventimiglia in time for the train leaving in the evening. I was walking along the Promenade des Anglais when a Mercedes drew up beside me and the driver leaned across and called my name. For a moment I could not think who he was, then I recognized Monsieur Zimdin's chauffeur. I had always liked him and I was glad to chat to him for a few minutes. Then he suggested that I should go and see Monsieur Zimdin.

'He's given up the apartment and he's living at the Negresco now. I'm sure he'd love to see you.'

Monsieur Zimdin! It all seemed so long ago. I had not thought of him for nearly a year. A year in which so much had happened. Yes, why not go and see him. Let the brute see me as I was – well dressed, self-confident, very different from the downtrodden little secretary who tolerated the humiliations for fear of losing her job. There was a spring in my step as I entered the doors of the Negresco, Nice's smartest hotel.

I went up to the porter's desk and asked for Monsieur Zimdin. The effect was astonishing. It was as if I had uttered some long awaited codeword to put an elaborate plan into action, or pressed a button to set some giant machine in motion. Things

83

moved swiftly, but above all discreetly. This was the Negresco and there must be no scandal. I must come quietly.

Come where, for God's sake? To the police station. The police station! But why, why? That you will find out soon enough. Get into this car.

It was annoying and distasteful. I would miss my afternoon's window-gazing and I had had quite enough of police stations lately. But clearly this affair was nothing to do with me. Evidently Zimdin was in some sort of trouble and I was mildly curious to know what it was – but not curious enough to sacrifice my pleasant afternoon for it. It was a bore.

I caught a glimpse of Monsieur Zimdin as I was hurried across a hall into an interrogation room. He was sitting slumped on a bench, his shoulders sagging, his mouth half-open, his eyes blank and bewildered. I did not feel sorry for him. This man had deliberately caused me suffering, he had enjoyed being cruel. But I did not exult at his distress. I was neutral, uncaring. Life had moved on since the time when Monsieur Zimdin loomed large on my horizons. He could not hurt me now and I had not the slightest wish to hurt him. He did not matter any longer.

I was brought into an office where a man sat behind a desk. The French police are not noted for their courtesy as a rule but I thought there was something approaching venom behind the barrage of questions this man shot at me. Who was I, what was my relation to Zimdin, how long had I known him, where did I live – every sort of question. It was all going to take a long time and I had to start out for Venice.

'I will answer your questions with the greatest of pleasure but first will you have the goodness to ring up a certain number,' I asked.

'I will do nothing of the sort. I wouldn't even think of it. What do you think I am – a public telephone?'

'What I think is that if you don't ring this number the consequences will be very serious for you.'

'For me! It's for *you* that the consequences will be serious!'

I think it was as much the stupidity of his tit-for-tat way of arguing as his hectoring tone which made me lose my temper. I thumped on his desk and shouted at him.

'For the last time I warn you. Ring this number *immediately*.'

He started to protest but thought better of it. Something in my manner must have convinced him that I was speaking with authority.

He asked for the number and then, unwisely, he said, 'Inspector Nivello here. Put me through to whoever's in charge.' There was a short pause and then he said, 'I have here a woman calling herself Edita Zukermanova.'

He got no further. I think it must have been The Admiral at the other end of the line. Nivello paled as he listened. He even rose respectfully.

'Yes sir. Yes, of course sir. Thank you very much, sir.'

He replaced the receiver and turned to me, smiling sheepishly. 'One of your officers will be here to collect you directly. In the meantime would you be very kind and tell me what you know about Monsieur Zimdin?'

'Very little. I worked for him for a few months but I really knew nothing of his affairs. What has he done?'

Inspector Nivello frowned. 'He may not have done anything. But don't you think it's peculiar? Here is this Russian who emigrates to Germany. When the Nazis come to power he leaves everything and moves to Austria. There he builds an enormous hotel, he owns a casino, he is very rich. And what happens when Hitler marches in? Zimdin flees to the South of France. He leaves all that and runs away. And he's not even a Jew! And here – look what he does here. He builds a most extravagant villa – really a fabulous place* – beside the sea at Eze with fuel tanks for his yacht. He collects precious stones. He flaunts tremendous wealth. Where does it all come from? Don't you find it peculiar?'

'Now that you mention it I do. I didn't when I was working for him – I assumed that what the chauffeur told me was true, that Monsieur Zimdin had smuggled jewels out of Russia.'

Nivello leaned across his desk.

'Do you know what I think?' he lowered his voice confidentially. 'I think he's paid by the Nazis to prepare a fuelling base for their submarines.'

I shrugged my shoulders. 'You might be right. But if you are, Monsieur Nivello, shouldn't you hand over your suspicions

* It was later owned by Greta Garbo.

to the Troisième Bureau? They are the anti-espionage department.'

Perhaps there was a touch of malice in my voice.

Before Nivello could reply the liaison officer from the Deuxième Bureau arrived to collect me. Sub-Lieutenant Roman was a young man of nineteen and he addressed as few words as possible to Nivello.

As we went through the hall Monsieur Zimdin jumped up from his bench.

'Mademoiselle Zukermanova! You remember me don't you? For God's sake help me! You know I don't speak French. I can't understand a word these people are saying. I don't know what they want. I implore you, telephone my solicitor and tell him I'm here.'

I turned to the Inspector.

'May I use your phone?'

'Of course, Mademoiselle. Of course. With pleasure.'

Then Roman chipped in. 'Monsieur Nivello will telephone the solicitor for you, and save you the trouble. Won't you, Monsieur Nivello?'

The whole afternoon was a squalid little experience from which I gained nothing. Except a demonstration of the antagonism which existed between the Deuxième Bureau and the police.

Chapter 8

It happened exactly as I had told Seraphin Ailhaud it would. The porter at the Excelsior referred to his book and wrote down my particulars without asking to see my passport. Koci came bouncing up, his bald head pink with excitement, and with a sly conspiratorial jerk of his head beckoned me into his office.

'We have a young Austrian aristocrat staying in the hotel,' he announced proudly. 'A very fine young man. Soon he will be called up for military service. I'm sure we could talk him into something. At least *you* could talk him into something.'

'We'll see,' I replied non-committally.

'He has booked a room for a month,' Koci went on. 'A little holiday before he goes to war. I'm sure that in a month you could . . .'

'Yes, yes. We'll see.'

At dinner that evening Koci gave me what he fondly imagined were secret signs to indicate his Austrian aristocrat. But his winks and his jerks were so obvious that the waiters exchanged glances and smiled to themselves. I could only hope that they thought that Koci was making an assignation with me. Georg von W... was fair haired and blue eyed, a handsome young man. He certainly did not look the sort who would fight with any enthusiasm for Nazi Germany and I decided to sound him out discreetly in the course of the next week. There was no need to hurry. Indeed it was a relief to know that there was no need to hurry over anything. I could stay in Venice as long as I liked and build a network slowly and carefully, taking no risks.

At nine o'clock two mornings later my complacency was brutally shattered by a thunderous banging on the door.

'Open. Police.'

As I grabbed my dressing-gown I tried desperately to think what it could be. I had taken no photographs, I had written no reports. The only thing I had done was to tell the Customs officers that the two silver fox furs and the Persian lamb coat were my own property and therefore not subject to duty. Even that was perfectly in order because I had not yet got round to selling them.

Two grave-faced carabinieri told me to accompany them to the *Questura*.

Koci was hovering as we passed through the hall but he was careful not to look in my direction. I could see that he was labouring under some deep emotion because his head was the colour of a tomato.

When we arrived at the police station I was told to sit on one of the hard benches and wait. It was an unpleasant experience. I had had no breakfast. In my haste I had forgotten to bring any cigarettes. I did not know what I was there for and consequently I could not prepare any defence. For nearly three hours I sat there, the bench getting harder and harder. I began to have sympathy for Monsieur Zimdin.

At last I was taken to see a senior police officer. He was standing behind his desk and I had hardly got into the room before he started shouting. Did I take him for an idiot? An imbecile? Foreigners were all the same – they thought they could get away with anything. On and on he went. Abruptly he ceased, and sat down. I remained standing.

He glared at me and I smiled back at him. What an unattractive creature he was, I thought, with his sallow complexion and his sharp little eyes. As he bent his head forward I could see that the hair was carefully brushed so as to conceal his bald patch. He took off his spectacles and holding them by one side, swung them round and round.

'You must think the Italian police are stupid! You come in here on a Czechoslovakian passport then next time you turn up with a French one. What are you playing at?'

So that was it.

'Nothing sinister in that,' I told him. 'My mother and I are refugees and now we live in Monte Carlo. I can't very well have a German passport when France is at war with Germany can I? Fortunately I have a great friend,' I lowered my eyelashes and simpered a little, 'who is a high ranking officer in the police, like you. Being so powerful and influential – of course you know how it is – he was able to get me a French passport.'

The officer twiddled his spectacles feverishly.

'But why do you come so often to Italy? Oh! Don't bother to lie to me. I know all about your entries from your previous passport – your genuine passport.'

'I see I must be frank with you,' I said.

'You'd better be,' he commented grimly, replacing his glasses.

'It's not very pleasant for me to tell you this. But my mother and I have so little money. So I bring furs into Italy and sell them.'

He stared fiercely over the top of his spectacles.

'Smuggling eh!'

'I wouldn't call it *smuggling* exactly. I mean they are my furs.'

'But you haven't paid duty?'

'No. Nobody has asked me to.'

'Why come all the way to Venice? You could just as easily sell your furs in San Remo just over the frontier, instead of travelling right across Italy.'

'Ah well, you see Josef Koci is an old friend of my father's. He lets me stay at his hotel in the off-season. When you're in my position free food and lodging is very important.'

The officer removed his spectacles again and twiddled them, faster and faster so that I thought they would fly out of his hand.

'What furs did you bring?'

'Always the same – two silver foxes and a Persian lamb coat.'

'And who are your customers?'

'I sell to furriers. I don't know how to find private customers.'

'Then you can't make much profit.'

'About a third. Anyway it keeps my mother from starving.'

He grunted and twiddled some more. Then he replaced the spectacles. It signified that he had come to a decision.

'All right. You can go.'

Koci was running round the hotel flapping his arms, his head glowing like a beacon. I tried my best to calm him down but without success.

'How did they know you had a French passport?'

This was something which had been worrying me too.

'I suppose the chambermaid must have seen it in my room and reported it to the police.'

Koci squawked in agitation and dismay. 'One of my own staff is spying on me! We are lost. We shall never be safe again.'

He was not a courageous man.

'We must never be seen together,' he insisted. 'Never. You will have to come to my room after I have gone to bed.'

I tried to imagine what Koci would look like in pyjamas. I could not.

'We can talk quite freely. My wife does not understand a word of German.'

He bustled away, and I went to the desk to see if there were any letters for me. There was one, from Mummy. It was, as always, sweet and loving but this time there was something different. She had met a most charming woman, nearer my age than her own, and she was sure that this woman and I would become friends. Her name was Erna Fiehl, a refugee like us. Her husband had escaped to England but she had her ten-year-old son with her in Monte Carlo. Mother was usually rather possessive, reluctant to share me with anybody so it was strange that she should have found a friend for me. It was almost as though she was prophesying that I would need Erna Fiehl one day.

The fuss with the police followed by my attempts to bolster Koci's flagging morale had been exhausting and that night I slept long and deeply. At nine o'clock in the morning came once more a thunderous knocking on the door.

'Open. Police.'

Oh! no, I thought, not again. But why? Had the officer changed his mind? Was he going to hand me over to the Germans after all? The carabinieri were silent, their expressionless faces betraying nothing as I accompanied them to the *Questura*.

This time I was not kept waiting but was ushered into the office. The officer was standing beside his desk but he did not shout. He smiled ingratiatingly which made him look, if possible, even more unattractive.

'I was kind to you yesterday, wasn't I?' he asked.

'Oh! yes. Yes, yes you were. Very kind.'

He took his spectacles off and examined them closely as if he had never seen them before. Then he gave them a twirl.

'And now,' he said, 'I want to ask you to do me a favour.'

Oh my God, I thought. This is it. How on earth am I going to get out of this one? I gulped and smiled as brightly as I could.

'I shall be delighted,' I forced the words out. 'What is it?'

He leered at me.

'Will you be very kind and sell me a silver fox fur for my wife?'

I soon struck up an acquaintance with Georg von W... and after four or five days I became convinced that he had no greater liking for Hitler and the Nazis than I had myself. He felt deeply the humiliation of Austria's position as a vassal state but he had no option but to join the army when his call-up became due. It worried him very much that he would be fighting for a cause which he despised against one in which he believed.

Very slowly and gently I sowed in his mind seeds of the idea that he might yet be able to serve the cause he thought right. When I told him that I could arrange for him to pass on military information to the Allies he recognized that it was his duty. It was a hard decision for him because he knew that his actions could result in the death of his own countrymen. I think it was the fact that he would deliberately be putting his own life at risk which finally convinced this proud man that it would be the honourable course.

I travelled back to Nice to consult the Deuxième Bureau about the best way for Georg to send on his intelligence and on the way I broke my journey in Milan and called on the Goldsteins. They had a miniature poodle, something of a rarity at that time. It was a bitch and it had recently had a litter of puppies. There were only two left, another bitch which the Goldsteins intended to keep and a dog which they offered to me. It was not difficult to fall in love with this little bundle of silver-grey wool with the bright eyes. I thought of the weeks and months during which I would be leaving my mother alone. I thought, too, of the four flights of stairs!

But in Vienna Mummy had always loved our fox terriers. She really would have welcomed grandchildren and she was at an age when she might have, in normal circumstances, expected me to provide them. Perhaps the little dog – his name was

Dougo – would be a substitute. It was thus that I rationalized my acceptance of the gift.

Mother met me at the station. She was, of course, delighted to see me but she could not help scolding me for bringing Dougo. How could she possibly keep a dog in one room in a hotel? Had I for one moment thought of having to get up in the middle of the night to take him out? Really, it was most inconsiderate. She simply could not think how I had come to do anything so irresponsible.

I did not take it very seriously. All the time she was scolding me she was cuddling Dougo and stroking his fluffy silver coat.

By the time we reached the hotel she had completely fallen under the spell of the little dog and she introduced him to Erna Fiehl with almost as much pride as she introduced me. Erna was all that my mother had said – beautiful, chic, intelligent and amusing. I saw a lot of her during my short stay in Monte Carlo and the more I saw the more I liked her.

It was soon after I returned to Venice that I had a strange experience. The walls of Koci's hotel were not thick and if people spoke loudly in the next room I could hear what they said. One night, quite late, I heard the heavy tramp of boots and two voices speaking German. Perhaps they were a little drunk and they were having an argument.

'I tell you it's the tenth of May,' one was saying as they came into the room. The other did not seem convinced. 'The tenth of May? I don't see how it can be. I mean how can it be fixed so far ahead? It's only November now. And anyway your head-quarters would keep it a secret if they knew. Which I doubt.'

'Oh headquarters! Yes they do think it's secret. But of course we all know. It's ridiculous.'

Then, bored with the subject, they turned to other things.

I lay awake wondering what it was that was planned for the tenth of May. Something military because they had talked about 'headquarters'. Two German officers on leave, no doubt. But what could it be that was scheduled half a year ahead?

Suddenly I had a strange experience. It was as if I were detached from myself altogether, a dispassionate observer. I was fully awake. It was not a dream, not a trance. It was more like a state of suspended animation. I stopped wracking my brains for the answer to the question: what would happen on the tenth of May? For I knew. I knew with utter certainty. On the tenth of May the Germans would launch their attack on the Maginot Line.

That the Germans would attack in the West sooner or later was almost taken for granted. Not that it worried us very much. We knew that France's Maginot Line was impregnable. This tremendous fortification, its roots deep in the earth, its branches bristling with the most powerful guns in the world, could not be beaten down. Everybody knew that. What everybody did not know, of course, was that the fortifications stopped short leaving a gap along the Belgian frontier.

When the attack did come it was not against this impenetrable Maginot Line. The Germans simply walked round the end of it.

But, lying in that little hotel room, I could have no idea what shape the attack would take. All I knew – but knew with complete conviction – was that it would start on the tenth of May.

I had had a similar experience years before, when I was at school in Switzerland. My mother had come to visit me and my father telephoned from Vienna to tell her that Grandmother was dead. She had been ill for a long time and the news had been expected any day. Mummy was sad but she had never been very close to her mother and nor had I. It was Grandfather to whom we were both devoted.

I simply did not believe that it was Grandmother who had died. I *knew* it was Grandfather. So strong was my conviction that I insisted on travelling home with Mummy. When we arrived we were told that it was indeed Grandfather who was dead. My father had thought it best to delay the distress we would inevitably feel until we were safely at home. To do so he told a lie.

On both occasions there had been the same certainty.

I lay awake for a long time considering what I should report. If I simply told the Deuxième Bureau that I had heard two German officers discussing something that was going to happen on the tenth of May it would be of no interest at all. But was I justified in relating the conversation to the German attack on the Maginot Line simply on the strength of a hunch?

'A hunch'. What is a hunch? To me it is something which comes from the unexplored corners of my mind. I know no more than that about its origin. But I do know that it can be relied on absolutely. It is the Voice of Truth. It was rare for me to have an experience of such certainty. It has happened only three or four times in my whole life. 'Intuition', 'sixth sense', which is something quite different, is with me most of the time. In fact it played so great a part in my career as a secret agent that it is difficult for me to tell where intuition ended and guess-work began.

But my certainty about the tenth of May was not intuition. It was clear and definite – black and white without any shades of grey. Also, of course, it was completely outside my terms of reference. I had no right to pass on as a fact something which the Deuxième Bureau themselves would, if they knew its origin, consider to be fantasy.

In the end I decided on a compromise. I would tell them that the German attack on the Maginot Line would take place on the tenth of May but I would qualify it by giving it the lowest grade of attribution 'I hear' rather than the stronger 'I see' or the most emphatic of all 'I know'.

I spent almost the whole of the winter of 1939/40 in Venice. The social conventions were much freer there than in Sicily and I was able to go about alone without being conspicuous. It was not necessary for me to have an escort and in fact after Georg von W... returned to Vienna I had no special friends. Le Petit provided an address in Switzerland for Georg to send his reports to. I never saw him again but I heard much later that he continued to send information for the rest of the war.

There was plenty of information flooding into Venice in that period which the British were calling 'the phoney war'. Although since the collapse of Poland there had been no fighting on land beyond a few light skirmishes between patrols, there was a great deal of troop movement. Besides which many Germans were coming to Venice on leave. So Koci was kept busy bringing me the tittle-tattle from the bars and bistros.

My mother wrote regularly. Little Dougo filled much of the letters but there was other news as well. Erna Fiehl had decided not to go back to Paris but to remain in the South of France to be near us – rootless refugees together. I could tell from the letters that she was settling down much better now, making friends and establishing a life for herself. On most days she would go to the Casino. She did not gamble. Her only game – and one at which she excelled – was poker and there was no poker game in the Casino at Monte Carlo. The attractions there were reading and refreshment rooms where she met other refugees from Czechoslovakia and Austria and one great asset was that the Casino had kennels in the basement where clients could park their dogs. Needless to say, the attendant in charge paid special attention to Dougo.

From time to time I would go back to report and it was a delight to see what a difference the little dog had made to Mummy's life. He was an absorbing interest to her and she lavished boundless affection and care on him.

When I was in Monte Carlo I never missed an opportunity of going to see my Algerian fur merchant and stocking up with a couple of silver foxes. They had stood me in good stead once and they might be needed again. Besides, my fur trading made a welcome and steady addition to our income.

Life had settled down to something of a routine for both of us, with occasional dramatic interruptions. One such was when Dougo developed distemper. Mother's letters became scrappy – and frantic. It was very serious. The vet did not expect him to live. He was so weak. He could eat nothing.

Then gradually a note of hope crept into the letters. Dougo was taking a little egg whipped up with brandy, from a spoon. He was holding his own, he was getting better. He was still very weak but the vet was sure the worst was over.

My mother's devoted nursing pulled the puppy through and in the process he became a very spoilt poodle indeed. On one of my trips to Monte Carlo I was amazed to see that Dougo, now fully recovered, still insisted on being fed. If I put his dish on the floor he would not touch it however much I coaxed him.

It was not until Mummy picked him up, tied a napkin round his neck and set him on her lap that he would graciously consent to take food from a spoon.

When I returned to Venice Koci winked and nodded more vigorously than ever. Evidently he had something unusually important to tell me. So, soon after dinner I tapped on the door of his bedroom. Koci was in the habit of getting up very early in the morning so he always retired directly after leaving the restaurant.

I found him sitting up in bed sipping strong black coffee from an enormous mug. Did it not keep him awake? On the contrary, it helped him to sleep. I need not have troubled myself to imagine what Koci would look like in pyjamas. He wore an old-fashioned nightshirt. Mrs Koci came in several times but if she minded finding a girl in the bedroom which she shared with her husband she showed no sign of it. Koci had probably told her that he was engaged in some currency deals with me or something of that sort. We did not need to interrupt our conversation – always in German because Koci's Italian was so bad – for she understood not one word of any language but Czechoslovakian. In any case I doubt if she would have been interested. She was a typical Czech peasant, closer to the soil than was her husband – and closer to the soil than to her husband.

Koci unfolded a strip of linen and held it out to me.

'What do you think of that?'

I looked. On the linen was drawn a cigar-shaped object. It seemed to be divided into compartments each of which was filled with closely packed writing. The ink had run a little so it was hard to make it all out. There were also several wine stains.

'What on earth is it?'

'It is a new German miniature submarine. Only seventeen metres long. Just think! A seventeen-metre submarine. They could have it in the North Sea one day and bring it by rail to the Mediterranean the next!'

'Wonderful, Josef. Well done. However did you get it?'

Koci swelled with pride and took a big gulp of coffee.

'Two German sailors in my bar. I got talking to them, the way I do. They told me they were on leave from Hamburg before their new U-boat was commissioned. I asked them – discreetly you understand – about it. I plied them with wine,' said Koci proudly. 'I spared no expense.'

'But why did you get them to draw it on this towel or whatever it is?'

'It is not a towel. It is cut from a tablecloth. One of my tablecloths. One of my *best* tablecloths.'

96

Edita Zukermanova

Edita's mother

Madame Gauthier

Dougo

His head glowed at the recollection.

'There was no paper handy. If I had left to fetch some they might have thought better of drawing their pocket submarine. Or they might have fallen asleep with their heads on the table. So I decided that I must sacrifice my tablecloth.'

I congratulated him warmly but I did not think that the information was very important. For me, one submarine was much like another. But in fact Koci's tablecloth, when it reached them, was the first the French Navy knew about German submarines seventeen metres long.

So unimportant did I regard it at the time that I did not hesitate to take it through the Customs myself, wrapped round a pair of shoes. A piece of torn cloth is not a suspicious object, like a film, and although my luggage was searched as usual, Koci's tablecloth was not remarked upon.

'By the way, you know that report you sent about the German offensive being launched on the tenth of May?' said Le Petit when I gave him the tablecloth. 'We passed it on, of course, but it's funny no other agent has given us the precise date.'

'Probably nothing in it, then.' I did not want to be questioned about how I had obtained this particular information.

'Well, we shall soon know.'

It was the twenty-fourth of April.

'Not that it matters when they attack. They'll never get through the Maginot Line.'

My Algerian furrier produced my usual order and I returned to Venice. Koci had several bits of gossip and over the next few days I sent them off to the Deuxième Bureau, writing laboriously with lemon juice. Then, having nothing better to do, I took the silver foxes over my arm – it was too hot to wear them – and walked along to the furrier in the next street, the one who had bought all my previous consignments. But this time he would not buy at any price.

'Nobody wants furs with the summer coming on. And by next winter who knows what will have happened. Italy may be in the war. No, I'm trying to get rid of my stock, not adding to it.'

It was the same story at two other furriers I tried. I walked pensively back to the hotel. If I were to continue coming to Italy I would have to find some other cover to replace the fur smuggling.

Chapter 9

When I got back to the hotel Koci was hovering in the hall. He was in a state of high agitation, his whole face flushed. With his high Slav cheekbones and his turned-up nose with its flaring nostrils he looked like a little sucking pig.

'Ah, I've been waiting for you!' he exclaimed. Then he glanced round the empty hall with exaggerated caution and lowered his voice to a conspiratorial hiss.

'A very important Fascist has just booked in.'

I felt a shock of dismay though I was more irritated than frightened. It was like being out without an umbrella when a sudden shower comes on. I did not think I would get wet.

'So what?' I said.

Koci snorted with impatience.

'Don't you see what it means? He must have come for you. We are in great danger, both of us. My God!'

I wished he would stop talking and let me think.

'What's his name?' I asked.

'Castellani.'

'You're sure you don't mean Castellano? Colonel Castellano from Sicily?'

'No, no. Castellani. Look, here it is.'

He took the register from the desk and held it for me to see. I read 'Dino Castellani' written in a very firm hand and underlined with a flourish.

'It's not the same man. But how do you know he is an important Fascist?'

'Because of the badge he wears in his buttonhole. It's a black and white skull-and-crossbones. I've never seen it before but I've heard about it. It's only worn by men who took part in Mussolini's march to Rome. There aren't more than about sixty of them left and they're all very close to the Duce.'

Koci paused to see what effect his announcement was having on me. 'He's probably head of the Secret Police,' he added with relish.

I knew that Koci loved to dramatize any situation but this time he could well be right. The OVRA went about their sinister business more quietly than the Gestapo, they were more subtle and discreet. But they were just as ruthless and just as efficient. There must be quite a thick dossier on me from Sicily with a few pages added in Genoa.

This threat was not a product of Koci's imagination and I would have to tread warily. The need was for caution, not action. I must not let myself be stampeded into doing something rash.

I had become accustomed to living with danger. It was always there and I was always aware of it. I could never relax. I was like a dog with its ears permanently pricked, listening for the knock on the door, the scratch on the wall. Sometimes the danger would rush in on me, as it had in Genoa; sometimes it would recede, but it never disappeared entirely. At any moment I must be ready to face it.

Koci was still talking. 'This Castellani won't be in for lunch but he will be here for dinner. I'll give him a table in the corner so that he'll have to pass yours to get to it. Be in your place early and then you'll be able to have a good look at him.'

The information that Castellani would not be lunching at the hotel was ominous. The only possible reason for an important man to stay at a modest two-star hotel like the Excelsior was to enjoy the good Czech cooking of Koci's wife. The little restaurant had achieved a certain amount of fame and people who would not consider staying in the hotel often came here for the starchy boiled puddings and dumplings – all the forbidden foods. But if Castellani was not going to be in for lunch there did not seem to be any reason for him to stay at the Excelsior. The big hotels in Venice were almost empty in wartime so he could have gone to any of them. But he had not. He had come to the Excelsior. Either he was there for some special purpose or he was not as big a man as Koci had made him out to be.

I wished that I knew the significance of the skull-and-cross-bones badge, if indeed it had any. Koci seemed very sure but I never placed very much faith in his judgment. I wished there was somebody I could ask. The Deuxième Bureau would be able to tell me but there was not time to get in touch with them. This piratical emblem was a childish one and it did not seem likely that Mussolini would have chosen it to commemorate the first of his triumphs. Probably, I comforted myself, it was simply the badge of some harmless club.

However, when Castellani entered the restaurant that evening I had no doubt about one thing. He was unquestionably a man of authority. He might or might not be the head of the Secret Police but he was certainly head of something. As he strode past my table Koci was hopping about behind him, nodding and jerking his thumb. It was quite unnecessary. If I had seen Dino Castellani fifty yards away in a crowded street I would still have felt the aura of power which emanated from him.

He was tall for an Italian – well over six foot – and he must have weighed something like sixteen stone. He was beginning to run to fat. He walked quickly, with restless energy, head thrust forward and long arms swinging at his sides. He did not look at me as he passed my table.

He read the menu with great concentration and I was able to study his face. An interesting face, but I could not make up my mind about it. The brow was wide and high, and the black hair had no trace of grey although the man must have been in his mid-fifties. There was a suggestion of coarseness about the nose, long and straight but slightly bulbous at its tip, and the pores of the skin were enlarged. Two deep grim lines ran from the nostrils to the corners of his mouth which was strong and sensuous. The massive spade-shaped chin had an incongruous dimple in it. He gripped the menu with big, square-ended fingers. Altogether he looked a tough, ugly customer.

When I am in a dangerous situation my impulse is to go out and meet it. This is not bravado. Several times in the past I had found that the shock approach saved me. I determined to use it now. I would speak to Castellani as soon as dinner was over.

Suddenly he uttered a bellow of rage. Koci ran to his table and bent his head obsequiously. I was too far away to hear what it was all about, but Koci grabbed the offending plate and scuttled out with it. A few moments later he was back with a fresh one, and Castellani grunted grudging approval. The little scene was quickly over but the sudden fury had shown me, if I did not know it already, that this thug was a very dangerous creature.

I spun out my dinner as long as I could, watching Castellani from the corner of my eye. He ate quickly, and when he had shovelled in the last mouthful he pushed his chair back and jumped up. I slipped from my table and we reached the door together. He stood aside to allow me to go through first, and I smiled at him.

'They serve coffee in the lounge,' I told him.

He nodded, and followed me in. He was not an easy man to talk to. Usually I found men, particularly Italian men, only too eager to make conversation but with Castellani it was very heavy going.

'Do you ever go to the Casino?' I asked.

'Yes. I'm rather a passionate gambler.'

Anything less passionate than that flat statement would have been hard to imagine. I decided to risk a snub.

'Would you care to escort me tomorrow evening? I love gambling too but I hate going to the Casino by myself.'

He hesitated for a moment and then agreed. There was no actual hostility in his manner but no warmth either. After a few more stilted sentences I got to my feet. He rose politely.

'Shall we meet here after dinner tomorrow?'

'That will be fine. Good night.'

I went to my room and thought over the events of the evening. But I could come to no conclusion. One thing was clear – Castellani was not interested in me as a woman. Why, then, had he consented to take me to the Casino? The only answer I could find to that question was a disturbing one – he was going to take any opportunity which offered to keep me under observation. I would need to be on my guard with every word I uttered. I had found it impossible to guess what he was thinking. He had deliberately avoided meeting my eyes and this I found very worrying.

I spent the next day like any innocent tourist. I did not think I was being followed but I was taking no chances. In the morning I went to the Accademia and in the afternoon I trudged round the Doge's Palace. But the Titians might have been so many posters. I was far too preoccupied to give them more than an unseeing glance. The biting wind which had been blowing off the Adriatic for days had at last subsided, and I no longer had to brace myself against its buffeting as I turned out of an alley into one of Venice's little piazzas. Normally I would have joyously greeted the sunshine which dappled the crumbling stones as a promise that the long winter was ending, but on that day I was simply impatient for the sun to set and bring my confrontation with Castellani nearer.

At last it was time for dinner. Castellani walked past my table without a glance, and the meal was a long agony of apprehension. I imagined horrible things. Perhaps his investigations were already completed, and he would not need to speak to me again, still less spend the evening with me. Probably he had instructed the police to arrest me, either in the lounge while I was drinking my coffee or later in my room.

Koci did not dare to speak to me except to take my order, and I was thankful not to have to listen to his fears and speculations. My own were bad enough.

Somehow I got through the meal and went into the lounge. Castellani came in hours later. I suppose it was only a few minutes really.

He drank a cup of *espresso* at a gulp.

'Shall we go?'

As he spoke he looked me full in the face. For the first time I was able to see his eyes – the most remarkable eyes I have ever seen. Dark brown and luminous, they seemed to penetrate me utterly. And the expression in them was unmistakable. The strongest possible sexual message.

I stared back and my own eyes must have responded. I was completely under the spell of that searching, enquiring gaze. I felt drawn into something wonderful and at the same time terrible.

'Shall we go?' he repeated.

I nodded, and we walked in silence to the Casino. There was no need for speech. Those few seconds when we looked at one another established an intimacy so close that words were unnecessary.

I forgot my fears. I forgot the Deuxième Bureau. I forgot that this man was my enemy. All I was aware of was that he was a man and I was a woman. I cared. Not for France, not for Italy. I just cared.

At the Casino he gave no indication that he remembered the look which had passed between us. He played with deep concentration, his face impassive whether he won or lost. As far as he was concerned I might not have been beside him. He won a small amount of money – not much because he had not been staking heavily – and after a couple of hours he rose from the table and collected his winnings.

On the way back to the hotel once again we did not speak. But as we entered the doorway his hand brushed against mine. His touch had the same magnetic quality as his gaze.

Koci handed us our keys, and I muttered my thanks. Then, without looking round, I started to walk up the stairs. I knew with absolute certainty that Dino Castellani would come to my room. As I went along the corridor I tried to tell myself that what I was doing was madness. But the feeling bubbling up inside me was all the stronger for being a forbidden one.

I did not have long to wait.

It was cataclysmic. We were male and female and nothing else mattered. All the preliminaries were swept away. They were irrelevant. Neither of us felt the need to say 'I love you'.

It was like being swept along on the crest of a wave and not caring that the wave would break on the shore because we knew that another wave would come along. I had a feeling of eternity; I could fly and fly for ever.

For me involvement must be total. The souls must meet as well as the bodies. There must be no doubts, no difficulties. I could not be unhappily in love. For me, that would not be love at all. I could not be anxious and suspicious and remain in love. There must be complete fusion, and there was with Dino Castellani.

As my fingers caressed his back I felt the bumps and ridges of a series of scars and weals.

'How did this happen, Dino? Was it an accident?'

He uttered a short harsh bark of a laugh.

'Only an accident in that it didn't kill me. It was meant to. A man shot at me.'

'In the 1914 war?'

'No. A long time ago but not as long as that. I was one of

Mussolini's first bodyguards. I was with him when he made his famous march on Rome.' There was a throb of pride in his voice.

I shivered. My fears came flooding back. So Koci had been right about the absurd pirate's badge. Suddenly the possibility that Dino Castellani might be the head of OVRA jumped a threshold and became a probability. Almost a certainty. But I shut my mind to it.

The wounds on his back aroused a great surge of compassion in me. In a strange way they made him seem even stronger and more powerful. Indestructible. I felt as if he had been attacked while defending me.

'Oh Dino! How terrible!'

His lips twitched. 'No, not very terrible. When you're playing for high stakes you've got to be prepared to pay if you lose.'

I snuggled up against him, and caressed the ridges of the scars on his back.

'Even this?'

'It was worth it. At least,' he added almost to himself, 'I thought so then.'

With a sudden movement he rolled over and I gave myself joyously to him. He would protect me, for ever.

The next few days were a dream. Only the nights were reality, the reality of sublime ecstasy. In Dino's arms I felt utterly secure.

He spent as much time with me as he could – all those long nights – but in the daytime he would abruptly disappear, with no word of explanation. He never mentioned his work and this in itself was ominous. Our long intimate conversations ranged over so many subjects that it was unnatural for him never to mention what it was he did. But I, like him, was extremely circumspect. I never referred to military matters although I made no secret of my loathing for Hitler. There was so much I had to hide that I made a point of being completely frank about anything which I could, without risk, disclose.

To my surprise I found that Dino himself was less than enthusiastic about the Führer. He resented the way Hitler, the jumped-up corporal, aped his own hero Mussolini. The uniform, the marching, the salute – the Fascists had them all first. And then this upstart came along and usurped them. They had had an ideal, bright, shining and clean. The Nazis had stolen the coinage and debased it.

'I often regret,' said Dino, 'that it was necessary for the Duce to ally us to the Germans. Don't forget I was in the last war fighting against them. And, well . . .' he shrugged those great broad shoulders. 'Perhaps I'm too old a dog to learn new tricks.'

But whatever the old dog's doubts about the new tricks he had none about his master. His loyalty to Mussolini was undiminished.

Over and over again he told me that Mussolini was too big a man to be swayed by Hitler. He did not disagree that Italy would soon enter the war but he insisted that it would be at Mussolini's bidding, not Hitler's.

'The Duce knows what's best for us,' he repeated. For him 'Mussolini is always right' was not just a graffito to be scrawled on a wall. It was a declaration of faith.

'A people must be led,' Dino would say. 'It's part of Nature. Every flock, every herd, every pack – each one has its leader, the strongest, the finest member.'

His outlook was entirely materialistic. Italy, under the genius of Mussolini, had a right to rule lesser nations and if this could be achieved only by war, war there must be.

'But, Dino,' I protested, 'the Italians aren't warriors. They're artists. It's the culture they've given to the world over the centuries that they're renowned for. That's what counts. If the Romans hadn't founded a culture they'd be forgotten by now in spite of their conquests.'

But he would have none of it. Mussolini knew best. And if Mussolini calculated that Italy's destiny required war for its fulfilment he would not question the decision.

'I was one of the first to recognize his greatness,' he boasted. 'And look what he's done for Italy already. His victories in Abyssinia, the colonization in Eritrea and Libya. At home, too, he's done a tremendous lot for the Italian people.'

'Yes, it's well known that he's made the trains run on time.'

'You can laugh if you like. But you must see the punctuality of the trains is only symbolic of something much deeper. Mussolini has brought out all that's best in the Italian people. He's given us both discipline and dignity.'

'I don't know anything about that,' I rejoined. 'But what I do know is that the heritage of a race lies in its culture. That's the quintessence of the past, it is the culture that remains. We talk about the twenty years of Pericles's rule as the cradle of culture – the Golden Age. That's what we remember – not the Spartans. And it's the same with the Romans as it was with the Greeks. Modern Italy is heir to the Romans.'

'Modern Italy is Mussolini's Italy,' Dino replied firmly. 'He's moulding us in his own greatness. He's even managed to raise the moral tone of the country. You don't see people kissing in the streets any more. It's forbidden. He's given us self-respect. We're no longer servile. In the old days someone would say to me "Dino, how is he?" It sounded humble, cringing. Now the same man would say "Dino, how are you?" More forthright, more direct. The Duce has abolished speaking in the third person.'

'That certainly makes it easier for foreigners like me to speak Italian,' I said lightly, and steered the conversation into other channels.

Quite casually Dino mentioned that he had a wife.

If I had known before that Dino was married I might have acted differently. But now it was too late. I was too deeply involved to stop. All my defences were down. All my principles were swept away. No moral considerations could be allowed to interfere with our love.

Not that Dino's wife posed any danger. Dino had grown far apart from her. The young and pretty girl whom he had married had remained provincial and now in middle age her ankles were as thick as her accent. Dino, ambitious, ruthless, dynamic, had forged ahead and left her a long, long way behind. So far behind that now they were out of sight of one another. All that was left of the youthful sweetheart was a good plain cook.

When Dino spoke of his wife the fire in those eyes would dull. He was heavy, cumbersome, plodding, hopeless. It was my joy that I had the ability to rouse him, to set leaping the flames which had been sullenly smouldering for so long. Together we would go whirling passionately to the heights, inseparable, invincible, soaring hand-in-hand.

But beneath it all I knew that my lover was a deeply disillusioned man.

Chapter 10

March 1940

It could not last, of course. In a day, a week, a month, Dino
would have to go back to his life and I would go back to mine.
We would be ranged against one another. Enemies. Enemies –
who had been so passionately, wonderfully, lovers. I refused to
accept the hideous realization and plunged ever deeper into the
moment. In my fantasy I believed it would be prolonged into
eternity. I glided into complete trust, confident that we would
live together for ever in our beautiful dream. There would be
no bitterness at the bottom of the cup.

We were strolling in the Piazza San Marco, the greedy
pigeons hopping out of our way at the very last minute, when
Dino looked at his watch.

'Come on. Back to the hotel now. I must pack.'

I halted and clutched at his arm.

'*Pack?*'

'Yes. I'm going to Rome this afternoon. Oh don't worry. I'll
be back in ten days or so. But I've been away too long already.
In these times it doesn't do to leave one's place empty. It's a
temptation to others to try to step into it.'

There was no point in arguing. Dino had made up his mind.
Nor was he a man for lingering farewells. I stood and watched
as he folded his clothes and laid them neatly, swiftly in his smart
suitcase. He would not let me help. But he did allow me to come
with him to the station.

On the *vaporetto* our conversation was matter-of-fact and
trivial. But once on the platform there were none of those
stilted exchanges desperately manufactured to fill a long and
agonizing wait. Dino had allowed exactly the right amount of
time to catch the train without delay or haste – the train which
he knew would start with the Duce-dictated punctuality.

As the long *rapido* pulled away from the platform he leaned from the window and waved. I waved back until he was out of sight. Then I went back to the hotel. Koci, his eyes bulging with curiosity, tried to waylay me in the hall but I hurried past him.

That night I lay staring at the ceiling, trying to sort my thoughts into some rational form of order. Without the effect of Dino's great dominating presence to overshadow everything I found it possible to look the facts in the face. But what were facts and what imagination? That Dino loved me was a fact. That he was a high Fascist official was a fact. (That he was head of the Secret Police was not a fact, only a very strong probability.) That I loved Dino was a fact. That I was a member of the French espionage service was a fact. That Italy and France would soon be at war was only a very strong possibility – almost as strong as the other. That France was already at war with Italy's Axis partner Germany was a fact.

There could be no future for Dino and me together.

But could we just part? As lovers, yes. But as enemies? I looked squarely at the realization that if he knew I was an enemy agent Dino would not let me go. I tried to tell myself that a man who loved me as Dino loved me could never bring himself to harm me. And when I was in his arms I believed it. But now, lying there alone, I knew it was not true. If Dino discovered that I belonged to the Deuxième Bureau he would never let me escape.

I knew that a man is capable of dividing his mind into water-tight compartments. That when love and duty conflict he can, without any feeling of hypocrisy, pursue two diametrically opposing courses at the same time. Dino would destroy me. Without hesitation. Without mercy. But he would never cease to love me.

The fact that he had complete control over his emotions only made me love him and admire his strength the more. My own emotions were utterly out of control.

In a curious way it was a relief to be able to accept that Dino could bring himself to destroy me. It made me prepare myself for the battle, if the battle should come. I would not submit meekly. I would put up a fight. I would be resolute.

Then gradually – and to my own astonishment – I found

that I could bring myself to destroy Dino. The position would need to be desperate to bring me to such a pitch. But if Dino opened an attack on me I would retaliate – and I would go on and on until Dino was destroyed. For the very first time I understood the fierce passionate battle of opposing interests which prompted Delilah to destroy Samson.

The realization gave me comfort. I knew that I had been behaving irresponsibly. The Deuxième Bureau had sent me to Venice to gather military information. All I had done was to become involved in a madly exciting and madly dangerous love affair. The sheer folly of it was inexcusable. But now that I knew that I could steel myself to betray Dino my sense of guilt towards the Deuxième Bureau vanished. At the same time my sense of guilt towards Dino was almost overwhelming.

Then another thought occurred. Perhaps Dino would never come back. Perhaps he had come to the conclusion that, because this clandestine affair would have to end some time, it was better to end it now. Perhaps he had slipped away. Perhaps he had found out that I was a French agent and to save me he had gone away pretending ignorance. No, Dino would not have done that. Nothing as easy and as cowardly as that. Perhaps – oh perhaps anything. My thoughts went round and round and came to no conclusion. I was no longer in control of events. I waited miserably to see what would happen.

One moment I knew Dino would never return. The next I was certain that he would.

He did. Not after 'ten days or so' but after five.

It was soon apparent that something serious had happened in Rome. Dino fell into long silences. He looked older, careworn.

'I can't stay long,' he said. 'I shall have to go back after the weekend.'

That night he said nothing about his five days in Rome and I did not dare to ask.

It was not until the next day, as we were strolling along the Riva degli Schiavoni, that he suddenly stopped beside a bench.

'I want to talk to you. Let's sit down.'

I waited for him to speak. But he sat silent, his shoulders hunched, watching the traffic of the gondolas on the Grand Canal.

'Do you know how Fascism got its name?'

I was taken aback. It seemed such an odd question.

'Well, yes,' I said. 'From the Italian word fascio. It means a faggot, doesn't it? A bundle of sticks.'

'Near enough. Go on.'

'Isn't there an old fable? Indian, I believe. About a king who said he would leave his kingdom to the son who could break a bundle of sticks.'

Dino nodded. 'That's right. Go on.'

I told him how the eldest son, a big strong man, put the bundle across his knee and tried to break it. He could not. Then the second son, also a big hefty man, tried jumping on it. The bundle of sticks remained intact.

'And then the third son came along. He was just a boy. He picked up the bundle and drew the sticks out one by one. He snapped each of them until there was nothing left of the bundle.'

'Yes,' said Dino slowly. 'Yes, that's Fascism. And I was one of those – and there weren't many of us – who helped to tie the bundle together. And now,' he said bitterly, 'I find that I'm tied up in the bundle myself.'

Then it all came out. Mussolini would not listen to Dino any more. The old dog could not learn the new tricks and his master was petting the young puppies while he growled in a corner.

'Everything was fine until this pact with the Nazis. We had built Italy up. Hospitals, roads, schools. Oh I daresay some people got hurt. We were in a hurry. We hadn't time to be gentle.

'And then this happened. The Duce was badly advised. He did an about-turn. We had troops on the Brenner, you know. We could have stopped the Nazis going into Austria. Dollfuss was the Duce's friend.'

Dino told me of his disgust with this Axis Pact. A German victory could mean defeat for Italy. Italy would become subject to Germany as Austria had.

'Anyway I don't believe the Germans will win,' he finished. In his ruthless way Dino was a straightforward man and the deviousness of politicians was distasteful to him. He had started out with a sort of rough idealism and now everything had turned sour. It was an astonishing outburst. Particularly for a man normally so reticent, so wary, so careful of what he gave away.

When he had finished he sighed and slumped back.

'It did me good to get all that off my chest.'

He leaned forward and, thinking that he wanted to walk on, I started to get to my feet. He pulled back.

'Not yet. I want to ask you something.' I looked enquiringly at him. His grip tightened on my wrist.

'Do you know anyone in the Deuxième Bureau?' he asked.

I had never completely lost sight of the fact that my lover was my enemy. That the time would inevitably come when we would do battle. But never had I less expected it to come than at that moment. As Dino had been pouring out his secret thoughts, utterances which his Fascist compatriots would regard as treason, I had trembled for him in case he should be equally indiscreet in front of anybody else. I was entirely off my guard.

But although you cannot make love with a sword in your hand you can keep it beside the bed ready to pick up at the first sign of danger. And now that sign had come, as I had always known it must. Although my whole body was tingling with excitement I forced myself not to show it. Slowly I turned my head and opened my eyes wide. I even managed a puzzled frown.

If Dino had hoped to shock me into a confession he would have phrased his question differently – 'whom do you know in the Deuxième Bureau?' or even made a flat statement – 'I know you are in the Deuxième Bureau'. That he did neither showed that this was his first shot in the battle but that it was not intended to be a direct hit. I took it for a warning shot across my bows.

'Deuxième Bureau?' I echoed.

'Yes, yes,' he said impatiently. 'The French Secret Service. Do you know anybody in it?'

I shrugged my shoulders and shook my head. When I am given a role I am not an actress playing a part. I live the role. I am it. I did not need time to think what answer I should give. If I had been a more polished performer I might have behaved differently. As it was, my very inexperience was my best weapon.

'Edita, this is serious. You know I love you. The one thing in the world I want is to spend the rest of my life with you. In Italy that would be impossible. I haven't told you but I'm in the Government. That puts it out of the question. But I've got a plan for us. It all depends on whether you can put me in touch with the Deuxième Bureau.'

I pretended to think for a moment.

'Well, I'm pretty friendly with the Commissaire de Police at Beausoleil. Would he know whom to contact, do you think?'

'Certainly he would. But whether he would put you in touch with them is a different matter.'

'Oh I don't think that's much of a problem. I'd make him realize that it was important. He'd do it all right. He's a very old friend.'

'Good. Go to Beausoleil tomorrow.'

'It wouldn't be any use. I happen to know he's on leave — I met him just before I came to Venice and he mentioned that he was due for some leave. He won't be back for about ten days.'

Ten days would give me ample time to get in touch with the Deuxième Bureau and obtain instructions from them.

'That'll do,' said Dino. 'It'll have to.'

My excitement bubbled up into a laugh of pure joy. Here was proof of the man's greatness. I had always known that he would find a way for us to live together. He could do anything. And I was his. And ten minutes earlier I had thought he was about to challenge me.

'Dino, what's your plan? Tell me.'

'You and I will settle in France together. For this we shall need money. I've worked it all out and I estimate that we shall need three million francs.'

Three million francs! It was more than a fortune. It was inconceivable. My mind just could not comprehend such a sum. I had always hoped that one day I might be able to afford a Citroën which cost ten thousand francs. But that day was far off — ten thousand francs was an impossibly large amount for me. And here was Dino talking about three million!

'But Dino, how on earth could you get three million francs?'

'From the French Government. I can sell the Deuxième Bureau the Italian Naval Code.'

I sat back on the bench and closed my eyes. It was the most wonderful moment. The Naval Code was any country's most closely guarded secret. A fleet which possessed the enemy's Naval Code would have the most tremendous advantage. A war-winning advantage. To gain Italy's Naval Code was something I had never hoped for even in my most extravagant

Dino Castellani

Italian Armistice Delegation, Hotel Chateaubriand, Hyères
(Admiral di Giamberardino in centre)

Croco Taudu

Edita Zukermanova
(Identification photograph
held by OVRA)

fantasies. All my sense of guilt towards the Deuxième Bureau fell away. It was the greatest espionage triumph ever known. And I had done it.

'But you will have to handle the preliminaries,' Dino went on. 'Go and see your policeman as soon as he gets back. When you tell him what it's about he'll put you in touch with the Deuxième Bureau. That is if you can convince him that it's genuine.'

'I can do that all right. I told you, he's a very old friend. But how am I to convince the Deuxième Bureau if I do manage to get in touch' – I phrased it that way because in spite of my excitement I was still cautious – 'that you really can get hold of the Naval Code? They may never have heard of you.'

'They have,' said Dino grimly.

A German sailor strolled past, an Italian girl beside him. Dino was silent until they were out of earshot.

'I must go back to Rome again tomorrow. It's very important that I shouldn't alter my routine or do anything suspicious. They'd shoot me, you know. They'd shoot me as a traitor.'

He squared his shoulders.

'I'm no traitor. The best thing that could happen for Italy would be if the Allies beat the Germans. And I think they will. There are many Germans – good patriotic Germans – who are waiting for the chance to bring Hitler down.'

Suddenly he swung round and stared at me. Those eyes were hypnotic. I felt they were dragging every last secret from the hidden corners of my soul. His face was set hard. But his voice was soft as he murmured, half to himself :

'This is no sudden impulse. Not just a middle-aged fool at the dangerous age chucking up everything to go off with a girl half as old as himself. No, not like that. It's been building up slowly, like a hairline crack in a dam. It stays like that for months and then suddenly in a flash the whole dam gives way and the water gushes out. Set free !'

For the four days that Dino was in Rome I was careful to do nothing which was not entirely innocent. Without his great impressive personality beside me, blotting out all my powers of thought, I was able to consider the situation if not calmly at least clearly. For all I knew my every movement was being closely watched so that it was essential that I should do absolutely nothing to arouse – or to confirm – suspicion.

My brain was restless, conjuring up first this possibility, then that. The whole thing could be some ghastly trap. My thoughts threshed to and fro, seeking answers to the thousand questions which clamoured at me. What was Dino doing in Rome? Was he getting orders? Was he giving orders? More likely, that. But *what* orders? Would he really sell the Naval Code? And if he did would it be the real one? Was he even now setting up an elaborate organization to transmit false information in a code which he was planning to sell to us?

I longed for him to come back. I felt secure with him near me, happy with the protection of those broad shoulders. But as soon as he went away this great mountain of doubt and fear rose up in me. It was such a horrifying possibility, the power of this one man to jeopardize the whole future of France. For myself I knew I was only a pawn in this vast global game, in no danger because of no account. I was involved in something which was too big for me to comprehend, confusing and baffling. I longed for Dino to come back and comfort me. I longed for Dino to go away for ever and leave me alone. The hopes and fears raced round and round in my brain, the longing and the dreading.

But when he did come back all the doubts and misgivings were swept aside. With him near me I could believe everything he said. I was completely secure and it was all wonderful.

The Deuxième Bureau ordered me to return to make a full report. Even the stilted formal phrases, brief and compressed, conveyed an excitement, an urgency. Dino had been right – they had heard of him, there was no doubt about that.

I did not tell him of this message which arrived before his return. But I told him about my French passport and how Ailhaud had given it to me, I told him about the silver foxes. I wanted to appear – I *had* to appear – as open and frank as I possibly could without giving myself away entirely.

As soon as I mentioned the furs Dino suggested that we should go to Milan where he was sure he could get me a good price for them. Then perhaps we might go to San Remo for a few days. Not for long because Ailhaud would, he said, be back from his leave and we must waste no time in getting in touch with the Deuxième Bureau.

We stayed for one night in Milan, at a hotel near the station and it was here that the last vestige of my doubts was removed. I always awake slowly, opening my eyes just a fraction of an inch and lying quite still. I was conscious of Dino standing beside the bed looking down at me and on his face was such an expression of affection and contentment that I was utterly convinced. It could not possibly have been bluff.

I felt certain that his feelings for me were genuine. He really did want to spend the rest of his life with me. He was fifty-six years old and he felt that time was slipping away. He was disillusioned with his old life and he saw the chance – and was fully conscious that it would probably be the last chance – of happiness, of peace for his remaining years.

Dino was a highly intelligent man and he was also a realist. He faced the certainty that the Fascists and probably the Nazis as well would ruthlessly pursue him, would never give up until they had tracked him down. He calculated the risks and accepted them. If he defected he knew that we would have to live the rest of our lives with the knowledge that at any moment one or other or both of us might get a bullet in the back. He was in love with me but he did not let the fact blind him to realities. He knew precisely what he was doing and he thought it was worthwhile.

I shared the dream. But our attitudes were different. His love for me was gentle, steady and strong. Mine was a spurt of passion. I had been desperately insecure ever since I left Vienna – a little boat being tossed about on a stormy sea. And now suddenly here was an island jutting out of the water, a refuge. I clung to Dino psychologically as well as physically.

In San Remo I cast my harness aside and devoted myself wholly to the dream. The Deuxième Bureau? Let them wait. I did not bother to let them know where I was or when I would be back. I did not know, did not care. Oh God, let this go on for ever.

It was Dino who urged me to return. My friendly policeman would be back now. I must go and make contact with the Deuxième Bureau. We must be practical.

Yes, we must be practical.

'Dino,' I said. 'Give me something to show them. Anything.

Just so that they'll see that you're serious.'

Dino laughed. 'All right, if you insist. What do you suggest?'

'Oh I don't know. Anything. How about a plan of the defences of Genoa?'

For a moment I thought I had overdone it. A plan of the defences of Genoa was exactly what a professional secret agent would consider valuable. I had been a fool not to ask for something less important. But Dino drew it for me without a murmur, humouring me. Or was he humouring me? Had I myself baited my own trap?

'You'll have to be very careful getting this through the Customs.' The remark was uncomfortably near an echo of my thoughts.

I had a half-empty Guerlain scent bottle which, for safety in travelling, I kept in its original padded box. I took the padding out, folded Dino's plan to the exact size, laid it on the bottom of the box, refitted the padding and put the bottle back on top. Dino watched me, smiling.

I expected him to say good-bye to me in San Remo but he came with me in the train as far as the frontier at Ventimiglia. He showed a card to the Customs officers. They smiled, they bowed, they waved me through. They treated me ceremoniously, courteously as if I had been visiting royalty.

Dino stood on the platform, smiling, confident, happy. Rock-like. But for my part, as the train clanked and shuddered out of the station my heart was heavy. Dino saw my going as a prelude, I saw it as a finale. I did not think the matter would end well.

While I had been with Dino the tenth of May had come and gone but I had hardly noticed it. The German attack on the Allied armies had been awaited so long that when it did come it seemed an anti-climax. We who were far away paid little attention, concerned as we were with our own affairs.

Quite soon we could ignore it no longer. The news from the north became more and more disturbing. It would be all right, of course, but things were not going well at the moment. But not to worry. The explanations were comforting – the withdrawals had been for strategic purposes, the line was being straightened, the armies were regrouping.

It was against this background of worry and uncertainty that I waited while the Deuxième Bureau decided what to do about Dino. What had seemed to me the insuperable difficulty – Dino's demand for three million francs – was considered very reasonable ('we would have given him twice that if he'd asked for it'), nor was the change of identity a great problem. The French were quite used to false passports and changes of name. It was one of the rewards for joining the Foreign Legion and there were regular systems for doing it.

I was not told of the deliberations, the consultations between Nice and Paris, and it was not until the outstanding problem had been solved that I was sent for. Apparently what had been worrying them was the risk of losing one of their agents – me. They feared that it was a trap and if I returned to Italy the OVRA would be waiting for me. Something rather similar had been achieved by the Germans when they had lured a British agent across the frontier from Holland a few months previously.

I had arranged to meet Dino in Milan and the question was how to convince him that the French would keep their side of the bargain if I did not go myself. The arrangements could be described in a letter but if it were delivered by an agent who was unknown to Dino he would be highly suspicious. The answer which the Deuxième Bureau had found to this problem was simple. My mother must go.

When they first told me this I thought they had gone mad. There were so many reasons why the whole thing was crazy. She did not speak Italian, her passport was invalid, she knew almost nothing about the working of the Deuxième Bureau, she could not possibly carry out a negotiation. And, above all, if it was a trap she would fall into it. No, certainly she must not go.

Gradually, patiently, they countered all my objections. My mother did not speak Italian. All right, but Dino spoke French didn't he? And she at least understood French even though she hardly spoke it. Her passport – no problem, they would give her a French one. It was an advantage that she knew nothing, there would be no danger of her giving anything away. There was no question of anybody doing any negotiation. All she had to do was to deliver a letter. And if it turned out to be a trap she would be perfectly safe. What possible good could she be to

Italian counter-espionage? If they closed a trap on her she would merely be an embarrassment to them. No, there could not be any danger.

It was, of course, this last argument which convinced me. My mother herself raised no objection. If she found the prospect daunting she did not show it. She was only too happy to be able to do something for me. So, leaving me with meticulous instructions about the care of Dougo, off she went.

When she left I expected her to come back in three or four days. It was too much to hope that Dino would be able to come with her. He would have to slip across the frontier by some secret means of his own, by himself. But it would not be very long before I would be reunited with the two people I loved best in the world. Meanwhile I had been entrusted with what I am sure my mother regarded as her grandchild, Dougo.

The war news became worse, dramatically worse. But it was remote. On the Côte d'Azur the sun shone brightly and there were no uniforms. Nevertheless it was probable that the situation would change literally overnight. It could not be long before Italy entered the war. Then the bombs would rain down on those sunny seaside towns and there would be bitter battles in the streets. Monte Carlo, so near the Italian frontier, was a bad place to be.

Le Petit did not order me to go but he advised me to. There was no organized evacuation. I could take my time to pack. Lyon was the place to go. Halfway between the Germans in the north and the Italians in the south it would be as far as one could possibly get away from the fighting. It was not like going abroad – I could telephone the office whenever I wanted to, and they could telephone me. Though perhaps it would be better if I did not telephone the office too often. Madame Gauthier at the Hotel Alsace-Lorraine would act as liaison between us.

It is a strange thing that when I was in Italy, away from my mother, I was perfectly capable of coping on my own. But here in Monte Carlo it was she who had gone away and I felt helpless. The prospect of packing up our belongings – hers, mine and Dougo's – appalled me. Fortunately there was Erna. Like a capable elder sister she took charge and organized everything.

We took my mother's suitcases into Nice and left them with

Madame Gauthier – Mummy would automatically go to the Hotel Alsace-Lorraine when she returned. Then Erna and I went back to Monte Carlo to collect my few cases and her mountain of luggage.

I took a last look round the shabby little room which had been home for so long. It looked so bare, sad and impersonal now. On the wall by the door, fixed with drawing pins, was the card setting out the hotel rules and prices. I hunted in my bag for a pencil. When I found it I scrawled across the card, 'Dino – I have gone to Lyon'.

So certain was I that he would come.

We found a nice little hotel in Lyon and we booked a room with two beds, Erna and her son Hansi occupied one and Dougo and I the other. The mornings were chaotic. Hansi made a lot of noise and so did Dougo, jumping excitedly from one bed to the other barking shrilly. Every morning I telephoned Madame Gauthier for news of my mother and every morning it was the same. None.

I was not worried about Mummy. I had implicit faith in Dino and I knew that he would see that no harm came to her. Even when Mussolini declared war on France I had no fear for her. I was upset, I was impatient, but I was not worried.

I had expected Italian bombs to rain down on Monte Carlo and Nice but nothing of the sort happened. The Italian Army marched into Menton and halted there. That was that.

But there was no need for the Italians to do more. The Germans were doing all that was necessary. The news from the north became ever more terrifying with the Nazi tanks sweeping through Holland and Belgium and right into France itself. The great, the famous Maginot Line lay there like a stranded whale as the fighting washed past it. The Germans probably agreed with the French that it was impregnable. So they simply went round the end of it.

When it became clear that the Italians were not coming any farther it was an indication that the end of the war was near – Germany would soon finish off France. The whole situation was changing, shifting, worsening all the time. Even when there is no hope one goes on hoping. I simply could not believe that the French Army – *La Grande Armée Francaise* – could be beaten. And anyway *something* would happen. The Americans would declare war, the British would counter-attack.

In this maelstrom of disaster two thoughts continually swirled round my mind. What has happened to Mummy? What will Dino do?

The telephone rang. Mother was back. In Nice, at the Hotel Alsace-Lorraine. Yes, Le Petit says I can come back.

And Dino? No, she told me, Dino cannot come. It is too late now. Any day the Germans will win the war and there is nowhere in France where you and he could be safe together. Too late now, too late.

We settled down in the Hotel Alsace-Lorraine to await the end – Erna, Hansi, Mummy, Dougo and I. My mother often spoke of Dino. How kind he had been to her, how much he loved me. How he had taken charge of everything and sent her back through Switzerland. How sad he was that it had all ended, and ended in the way it had.

Then came the Armistice, that horrible day.

At first we thought that France must have been betrayed – a political coup of some sort. Defeat was unbelievable. At least for us, we who had never seen the streams of refugees, or heard the guns and the bombs and the clanking of the tracks of tanks. In Nice the sun still shone, there were no uniforms, no bombs screaming and whistling, no fires, no heaps of rubble where people's homes had been. Everything was outwardly normal, even the Casino reopened the day after Armistice.

How could we have been defeated? *La Grande Armée Française* defeated in three weeks? No, such things could not be. But they were. I think it would have been easier to bear if there had been any visible signs of defeat. If jack-booted Nazis had marched through the streets of Nice. If there had been corpses sprawling on the pavement, if there had been anything to show that a war had been fought and lost.

And not only was France defeated. I was defeated too. For over a year now I had been keyed up to a pitch of patriotism which found its outlet in my life. My missions had been expressions of my philosophy – crusading if you like. And now it was finished, all finished. Nothing more for me to do.

It was a terrible feeling. Le Petit came to the hotel but most of the time we sat in silence. There was nothing to say. He had the most expressive eyes, and now they were just huge dark pools of pain.

'What will happen?' I asked. I knew he could not give me an answer. 'I don't know. But something will happen. I don't know what but something. There is a God. Something will happen.' I spoke for the sake of saying something. When the silence became unbearable.

Neither of us believed it. We knew that in the end Hitler would be defeated, that we never doubted. But, it would be the British – and probably the Americans – who would do it. Britain could not be defeated. The prestige of Britain was unlimited, that mighty Empire. Everything English was so much better than anything made or done anywhere else; I had been brought up to believe that. Nothing like this could happen to England.

But it happened to France. It was as if somebody had told me that God did not exist any more – had *proved* to me that God did not exist any more.

It was like being buried alive. I was completely powerless, I had lost all purpose.

Most of the time I lay in bed, listless, not eating.

And when my mother and Erna persuaded me to get up and go out I put on the first clothes which came to hand, not caring what they were. I did not bother to make up my face or comb my hair. I shuffled along with my head bent, hating the mocking sunshine.

It had all happened with such dreadful suddenness – a miserable three weeks. If it had taken months it might have been possible to adjust one's thoughts to the possibility of defeat. But the brutal suddenness found one unprepared. It was a stupid nightmare. Just not possible. This Armistice and this defeat. But it *had* happened. The phrase hammered in my brain – it can't happen but it has. It can't happen but it has. There was no France any more.

Mummy and Erna tried to coax me back to life. Would I come for a walk along the Promenade des Anglais? No I would not. Would I take Dougo for a walk? No I would not. Would I come to the Casino? No I would not. Questions, questions, questions.

'Oh all right, all right, all right. I'll come to the Casino.' I watched dully, uninterested. Red, black, red again. Black.

All life was black. The impertinence of red. Black, black, black. Shall we go home? Might as well.

As we went out of the doors of the Casino I saw a figure running up the steps. It was Le Petit.

When he saw me he stopped. He flung out his arms. Those huge luminous eyes were shining like over-ripe cherries. Their whites were clear with a bluish tinge. Every muscle in his body quivered with excitement.

'*On Continue!*'

Chapter 11

July 1940

'We are going on!' It was the most stupendous news. So totally unexpected. It was like a last minute reprieve from a death-sentence – no, better than that. It was like rising from the dead.

But how? Why? France is defeated. Our war is over. How is it that we can start again? Such things are not possible. Is it true, is it true?

I pelted Le Petit with eager questions but he knew little more than I did. And that little he did not tell. I assumed that my great hero Admiral Darlan had authorized the continuation of the espionage organizations. For, after all, the French Navy still existed. With some of its ships sunk by the British to stop them falling into German hands, some of its ships bottled up in Alexandria, reeling under the humiliation of defeat, the French Navy still existed. Metropolitan France was crushed but French Algeria still remained free. The Pétain Government had signed an Armistice with the Germans but there were many French-men who did not consider that the Pétain Government had the right to sign for France. Their loyalty was to their country – they put France before any Government. To accept defeat was, for them, to accept dishonour. Some escaped to England to join General de Gaulle so that they could renew the fight. Others remained at their posts so that they could help their country from within.

One of the latter was Commandant Nomurat to whom Le Petit told me to report at the great naval base at Toulon.

'You'll be receiving your orders from him,' Le Petit told me. 'But I'll keep in touch and I'll go and see your mother from time to time.'

I was being lent to the Troisième Bureau – the counter-espionage department of the French Intelligence Service. They had already established secret channels of communication with the Allies. How and to whom I never knew. If I had asked I would not have been told.

Commandant Nomurat was half Japanese. His face was alight with intelligence and he had exceedingly delicate hands. If he was surprised that a woman should choose to be a secret agent, he was far too polite to show it. Before briefing me he insisted that any letters or papers I had should be handed over to him and locked away in his safe. The reason was that I had changed my name.

Immediately after the Armistice Le Petit had suggested that I should have French papers – identity card and ration card in a French name.

'How about Chabot?' he asked.

'All right. But what first name?'

'That's for you to choose. What would you like?'

'Marianne – the symbol of the French Republic. Marianne, of course.'

And so I became Marianne Chabot – my mother was Anastasia Chabot. Everything to do with Edita Zukermanova, anything which might connect Marianne Chabot with her, was locked away in Commandant Nomurat's safe.

I shed Edita Zukermanova as a snake sheds its skin. And with Edita went Dino. The opportunity had passed, Dino could not come now. It had been a fiercely passionate affair but it had been brief, brutally brief. It was like a sudden thunderstorm in summer. Intense while it lasted, now it was over.

For a few short weeks I had sheltered beneath the protection of Dino's rocklike personality. Now this rock had vanished and I returned, as I always did, to the loving shelter which my mother provided. It is not my nature to repine. Even as a child when a favourite doll got broken, I immediately lost interest in it.

Satisfied that the remains of Edita Zukermanova had been interred in his safe, Commandant Nomurat gave me my new mission. It sounded interesting.

The Germans had occupied Paris and the north. The Italians had occupied only Menton in the south but they were going to establish an Armistice Commission – what today would be called a 'presence' – near Toulon, more or less halfway along the south coast of France. A hotel at Hyères, the Châteaubriand, was being put at their disposal. And the job?

'You,' said Nomurat, 'will be, shall we say, supervisor. You will see that the Italians are treated properly. They will bring their own servants but you will tell them where to buy things – see that the sheets and towels are changed regularly. That sort of thing. It's a perfectly genuine job but you will also pick up any information you can. People are careless about throwing things away – things they ought to burn.'

Rooting through wastepaper baskets was a sad comedown after photographing battleships in an enemy harbour but it was better than nothing. And living rent-free in a first-class hotel without having to bother about rationing and shortages was a consideration.

The Hotel Châteaubriand was first class. Set in an enormous park and freshly painted a dazzling white it was most impressive. Its owners, Swiss citizens whose name was Joeriman, had furnished it with antiques and the whole effect was one of restrained luxury.

The Italian Armistice Commission was due to arrive at two-thirty and would be greeted – if not welcomed – by a French naval officer and the Prefect. I spent the morning wandering round the hotel, examining the splendid rooms and memorizing the layout. The Joerimans, affronted at having their hotel commandeered for the purpose of housing the conquerors, had retired to a house in the park and I was alone in the hotel. Suddenly I heard the commander of the French naval guard who patrolled the building rap out a command. There was the rattle of rifles as the guard presented arms and the sound of cars on the gravel. I went out to see what the commotion was about.

Several cars drew up and on one I saw the insignia and flag of an admiral. Out of these cars emerged the Italian Armistice Commission and I stood watching in amazement. They were like something out of a glamorous film. In their snow-white uniforms liberally decked with gold braid they were magnificent, godlike. Each was more handsome than the next, an élite band of Italian manhood.

I stepped forward, smiling. The Admiral bowed and kissed my hand. Then he turned to the staff grouped round him.

'How French!' he said with a smile. 'No other nation would think of anything so charming. As a reception committee just one beautiful woman.'

With that remark he set the tone of his Commission. Admiral di Giamberardino was no Fascist. He had fought beside the French against the Germans in the First World War and he carried out his duties with compassion and sensitivity. He had the soul of a poet and the looks of a god. Magnificent eyes, a Roman nose, a perfectly shaped mouth, his features might have been carved from marble by the hand of a master. He had an air of patrician elegance.

When the official French reception committee, hastily summoned by telephone, arrived, hot and flustered, he soon put them at their ease. He was one of those rare men who never had to assert his authority, secure in the knowledge that no one would ever question it.

At first the Italians were very careful and security-minded. They never left anything in their wastepaper baskets, everything was painstakingly burned. But soon they relaxed and, with the help of the chambermaid, I was able to salvage several items which proved to be of interest to Commandant Nomurat. I also overheard a few snatches of conversation which I duly reported. I think Admiral di Giamberardino guessed that I had been planted on his delegation because whenever German officers arrived to visit him he made a point of telling them that I spoke German, thus warning them to be careful what they said in my presence.

Commandant Nomurat decided to bug the Italians' radio traffic and he gave me a microphone to place in the room immediately above that in which they had installed their transmitter and receiver. But the Hotel Châteaubriand was solidly built and the microphone was not sensitive enough to pick up any sound from below.

Gradually, though, it became apparent that no worthwhile military intelligence could be found at the headquarters of the Italian Armistice Commission. It was a backwater – a very pleasant backwater – and the main stream of war flowed relentlessly past it. We lived a sheltered existence there and any news of war secrets which reached us were in the form of titbits of gossip, brought by visitors from the great busy world beyond the cool tree-shaded park where we lived in happy ignorance.

I developed a slow but firm friendship with Admiral di

Giamberardino. It was completely sexless, based on admiration and respect. A man as wise and as cultured as he was could never have been attracted by the strident calls of Fascism, still less by those of the Nazis. Nevertheless he was a patriot, a serving admiral, and his attitude towards his own country was one of utter loyalty. He had a way of sympathizing with me without agreeing with me. One day, during a long discussion, I suddenly burst out.

'I *hate* Hitler! I hate him, hate, hate him!' All the venom and frustration which had built up in me over the years exploded in those words.

Admiral di Giamberardino reproved me gently. 'No, no. Don't hate him. Don't hate anybody, ever. Every time you hate somebody it puts a wrinkle on to your beautiful face. No, no, don't hate people.'

I used to spend long hours sitting with him on the terrace of his suite discussing everything under the sun. Not since my father died had I had the guidance of a mature wise man and Admiral di Giamberardino became my mentor. For the sake of appearances he invented the pretext of brushing up his French so we spoke in that language in case we were overheard. In fact his French was not absolutely fluent and when he wanted to voice a compliment or one of his calculated indiscretions he would whisper in Italian.

But while my undercover work did not produce anything of any great importance I was kept extremely busy at my ostensible job. The Italians did not take kindly to the discipline of solitude and they quickly became bored. Where could they go in the evenings? What could they do? Which was the best restaurant on the way to Nice? What was on at the cinema in Hyères? Where could they get their nails manicured? For the answers to all these questions they came to me and I found myself running up and down the broad staircase all day long.

Then they asked me where they could buy presents for their wives and girl-friends. The victorious lira was mightily strong in comparison with the conquered franc so that what seemed expensive to the French was absurdly cheap to the Italians. The shopping lists became so long that it would have taken all my time to satisfy them, so I invoked my mother's help. She would come from Nice to Hyères, stay the night in the hotel, and depart with requests to find anything from antiques to furs, from scent to champagne.

On these expeditions she naturally would not consider being parted from her beloved substitute-grandchild, so Dougo came too. I did not quite dare to introduce him into the dining room, he was left shut up in her bedroom during dinner. Poodles are proud, and he would not suffer this indignity without taking revenge. When we returned to the bedroom we found that he had filled in the time by tearing up sheets. If he had been a Red Cross worker making bandages he could not have been more diligent. One of Madame Joeriman's precious linen sheets was destroyed utterly. Mummy, in the old and happy days, had been house-proud herself so she readily understood – and sympathized with – the horror with which Madame Joeriman would receive the news of this disaster.

'What can I do? What can I do?' my mother wailed.

I thought frantically. At last the solution came to me. Desperate situations demanded desperate actions. I ran up the stairs and into an empty room on the floor above. I whipped a sheet off the bed and rushed back to her room. It was not possible to conceal the loss of the sheet but I trusted that my subterfuge would direct suspicion away from the real culprit, unrepentant as he was.

My mother's shopping expeditions were a great success. So much so that before very long the Italians suggested that it would be more convenient if she came to live in the Hotel Châteaubriand so that they would not have to wait for a week or so between giving her their orders. This naturally suited us very well. We were together and also it saved us paying a hotel bill. It was a great satisfaction to us that after being ruined by the Nazis we were now being housed and fed by their Fascist partners. And not only Mummy and me but Dougo as well. For the first time since leaving Vienna we did not have to worry about money. We added a percentage to the price of anything she bought and the Italians were still delighted to get things so cheaply.

Except when there were Germans present we would spend the evenings with the Italians, playing bridge or billiards or table tennis. Sometimes we would invite some young girls, friends of the Joeriman's daughter, and dance to the gramophone. But whenever Germans came we made ourselves scarce. Our Italian friends told us about those evenings. After dinner they would move to the big salon. Then the servants would bring in champagne and hosts and guests would join in drinking interminable toasts. This was, I felt, not for us.

One day when she had gone on a shopping expedition to Nice I was sitting talking to Admiral di Giamberardino on his terrace.

'I'm entertaining some German officers tomorrow, two admirals and a general. They'll have their ADCs with them – it'll be quite a big party. Why don't you join us after dinner?'

I was astonished, and rather hurt.

'You can't ask me to do that. You really can't. You know how I feel about them.'

'But I *am* asking you.'

'You see,' I said, 'if you didn't know my feelings about the Germans I might have come, just to please you. But as it is I'd be horribly embarrassed. It would be against everything. You could almost say it would be against my honour.'

He smiled his whimsical smile.

'Trust me, my dear. Put on your most beautiful dress and come. You'll enjoy it, I promise you.'

'But,' I protested, 'what am I supposed to do when you drink all those toasts? You can't expect me to lift my glass and join in when you drink to victory and Heil Hitler and God knows what.'

He held up one of his slim elegant hands.

'Please, trust me. That's all.'

'All right,' I agreed reluctantly.

The Admiral jumped to his feet. 'Splendid. We'll have fun.'

I did trust him. How he would manage it I did not know but I was confident that he would see that I was not embarrassed. It was, therefore, with pleasurable excitement that I turned my attention to the question of what to wear.

I had one very special dress which was a model made for me in Vienna. It was a classical evening dress, long and graceful. Although it was now several years old I had had very few occasions to wear it and its style had not dated. The heavy material shimmered as lustrously as ever and just fingering its richness made me happy.

When the Nazis had come stamping and heiling into Vienna a woman we knew had asked us to look after her ermine cape for her.

'I'm going to America,' she announced, 'and I've got to travel light. I can take my diamonds sewn into my girdle but the ermine's too bulky. I'll leave it with you in the hope that we'll meet again some day. In the meantime if ever you get a chance to wear it for heaven's sake do. It'll only go yellow if you don't.'

When Mummy slipped across the frontier into Italy she brought the cape with her and now I saw an opportunity, the first opportunity, to take its owner at her word. It was a lovely thing, soft as velvet, smooth as silk, the little tails with their shiny black points etched against the gleaming whiteness. Stroking this lovely cape gave me confidence as I glided through the magnificent hall towards the large reception room where the company had gathered after dinner.

The double doors were open and several of the officers noticed me coming and stopped talking. Soon the others turned to see what they were looking at and all eyes were upon me as I made my entrance.

I was confronted by a dazzle of uniforms. They nudged one another and stared. Admiral di Giamberardino stepped forward, his eyes alight with amusement. He bowed courteously and taking my hand he turned to the German admiral standing stiffly beside him. The Germans were completely taken aback. The Italians less so because they knew me, but the Germans had been expecting a wholly male party. Who on earth was this woman? Beautiful, but who is she? The Italian admiral's mistress? Probably. Just what you would expect of an Italian. The Germans frowned fiercely. I could read their thoughts as I watched the expressions crossing their duel-scarred faces.

'May I introduce,' said Admiral di Giamberardino, 'La Contessa di Chabot?'

There was a clicking of heels and a shaking of hands. I progressed round the room with Admiral di Giamberardino beaming affably beside me. His whimsical joke would probably cost him his job when Mussolini heard about it. But what did he care? With traditions dating back to the Renaissance he was very much his own man. Dictators come and go but the di Giamberardinos of this world go on for ever.

'The Contessa has great talent. I don't know how she manages it but she speaks Italian like an Italian, French of course is her native tongue, and German she speaks – as you will see – like a German. Or, perhaps like an Austrian.'

He would not allow the joke to go too far. He still remembered to warn his guests to be careful of what they said.

This only added to their respect for me. They could not make me out but it was evident from Admiral di Giamberardino's manner towards me that in one way or another I was a person of importance. They did not know what it was all about but to be on the safe side they treated me with deference. As I floated round the room I hugged myself with joy. That I, their enemy, should have these high-ranking German officers clicking their heels and bowing to me was a supreme satisfaction. It was easy for me to smile at them and to incline my head graciously in acknowledgment.

By this time I had worked myself so much into my part that I really believed myself to be in a position where by a frown or a caustic remark dropped into the right ear I could blight the careers of these Nazi officers. I savoured, with excitement, the sense of power.

When I had completed my royal progress round the room I sank elegantly into the antique armchair which Admiral di Giamberardino pulled forward for me. I smoothed the rich folds of my dress and waited to see what would happen next.

The officers seated themselves and they were soon talking animatedly. Yet it was not a relaxed atmosphere. The Germans despised the Italians as fighters and the Italians knew it. But here the Italians were on their own ground and they knew that in matters of culture and art they were infinitely better equipped than their guests. So the Italians maliciously kept their conversation on a high intellectual level, the wit darting and sparkling while the Germans lumbered along hopelessly outclassed. Of course there was no open hostility – it was an animosity conducted with smiles. Admiral di Giamberardino sat with a bland expression on his face but I knew him well enough to be certain that he was missing none of it, and enjoying himself hugely.

Some of the Italian officers disengaged themselves and wandered up to compliment me on my appearance and to comment on that of the Germans – how ugly their close-cropped hair looked, how ill-fitting were their uniforms. They spoke – in Italian, naturally – without looking at their victims and so light-heartedly that the Germans never guessed that derogatory remarks were being made about them.

Soon it was exident that one of the German admirals was well aware of the game the Italians were playing. He had had enough of their teasing, of their flicking of venomous little darts with a light touch like picadors dancing round a bull. When one of the Italians remarked that Italy was the cradle of culture the German admiral smiled charmingly.

'Yes indeed,' he agreed. 'But let us not forget that the baby is more important than the cradle. And the baby had a twin, born in Germany. Both have the same name – Culture. But to distinguish them the Italians spell the name with a C. We spell it with a K.'

That effectively put a stop to the teasing. There was an awkward silence fortunately broken by the entrance of the stewards bearing champagne on silver trays.

Now was the moment when Admiral di Giamberardino's promise to me would be put to the test. As he rose to make his speech I looked at him as if to say 'Don't you dare try to make me drink to Hitler. If you do I shall hurl this glass against the wall.' He looked innocently back at me and I think an eyebrow twitched.

All the officers stood up and silence fell on the company. They looked expectantly at Admiral di Giamberardino, the Germans already frowning with concentration at the prospect of having to follow a long speech in French. Few of them spoke Italian but they all had a sort of schoolboy French.

Admiral di Giamberardino raised his glass with a sweeping graceful gesture and held it above his head so that the light from the chandeliers caught the bubbles and made them sparkle.

'*A la vie, a l'amore!*'

There was a stunned silence.

The Italians were the first to recover and they raised their glasses. '*A l'amore!*' they echoed.

The Germans simply could not believe their eyes and ears. To drink to love! It was unheard of, quite unheard of! But the conventions must be observed. They hastily gulped their champagne. '*A l'amore!*' they muttered.

Everyone looked again at Admiral di Giamberardino. Odd to have a toast at the beginning of a speech not at the end but, anyhow, that was what he had done. Perhaps because it was so flippant he wanted to get it out of the way before coming to the serious part of his speech. What would he say? Praise Germany, of course. Perhaps he would try to find something to praise Italy for. Hitler, Mussolini, one took it for granted that there would be praise for them. Then no doubt there would be another toast – a proper, solemn one this time. To victory. They cleared their throats the louder to shout '*Sieg Heil!*'

Admiral di Giamberardino waited until the room was completely silent before looking at each of the expectant faces. Then he sat down.

It was a moment before anybody realized that there would be no speech. No speech. Nothing.

The Italians had much more of a sense of humour than the Germans but even they were flabbergasted at his temerity. And I, although I was exultant at what he had done, was worried about the situation. I was fairly certain that among Admiral di Giamberardino's staff was a Fascist spy who would duly report the incident to Mussolini and I feared the consequences. But Admiral di Giamberardino had done it with his eyes wide open. The exquisite enjoyment he derived from it made the whole thing worthwhile, whatever the end might be.

In order to cover the awkward silence I proposed that we might dance.

'But who with?' asked one of the Germans.

'I'll sacrifice myself. I'll dance with each of you in turn. Starting with Admiral di Giamberardino.'

We danced a Viennese waltz, opening the ball so to speak. It was a glorious dance, the Blue Danube, and the Admiral and I fitted one another perfectly. We spoke not a word as we swooped and glided, seraphic smiles on our faces. The only communication we had was the pressing of hands, the touching of fingers. But it was enough. We understood. 'You see, I told you you could trust me,' Admiral di Giamberardino seemed to be saying and by a squeeze of his hand I answered that I had never enjoyed an evening more.

To dance with anyone else would have been an anti-climax.

We had some more champagne – no toasts this time – and a German general came and sat with me. He complimented me on my dress – as well he might. Perfectly plain, it relied upon the excellence of its cut. He asked me whether I had bought it in Paris and I told him no, Vienna.

'Ah Vienna. Do you like the Austrians?' he asked.

'No.'

'Nor do I. They are nothing. Nobodies.'

I did not remind him that his Führer was an Austrian.

'But the Czechs,' he went on. 'They're something different. Do you know, when we marched into Prague and the Führer was there they stood in silence. And as the head of the column reached them they turned their backs. It was a silent protest – there was nothing we could do. Oh yes, give me Czechs rather than Austrians every time.'

How I wished I could tell Koci what he had said.

It was now half past eleven and Admiral di Giamberardino was looking exhausted. Many of the Italians had melted silently away and at last the Germans made a move towards going to bed. As he stood aside to let me pass through the door the General caught sight of the ping-pong table.

'Is that what they call table tennis?' he asked.

'Yes. The English call it ping-pong.'

'Would you show me how to play it?'

'Of course, Herr General, with the greatest of pleasure. After breakfast?'

'No, no. I am leaving early. I meant now.'

So, in spite of the high heels of my silver shoes – which were by now getting uncomfortably tight – I showed him. The rules are not difficult to explain and I hit a lob towards him. With great precision he returned it and we developed a slow-motion volley. Ping – the ball arched over the net. Pong – back it came. Then I sharpened it a little and he missed.

Very carefully he analysed the shot. He puzzled over it until he was satisfied that he knew what he had done wrong. Then came the business of getting it right. He approached the game with the utmost solemnity. He was going to learn to play ping-pong and nothing was going to stop him. The fact that I was almost dying on my high heels did not signify with him. The stubbornness of that man! The seriousness with which he played!

It took on the aspect of a military campaign. His concentration was complete. If he hit the ball from that angle it would go there – if he hit it from this angle it would go there. Now he understood the game.

It was four o'clock in the morning before he was satisfied that he had learned to play ping-pong. Two and a half hours of utter single-mindedness had achieved the objective.

But nothing, nothing in the world, not even two and a half hours of ping-pong could spoil the magic of that evening for me. All the humiliations, the disruptions of my life, all the misery and hardship which the Nazis had caused me had been avenged. It was my triumph. And the fact that only I knew what a tremendous triumph it was made it all the more precious to me.

Chapter 12

May 1941

The Hotel Châteaubriand was an oasis, psychologically as well as physically. But from an oasis every caravan must move on, out into the hot bare desert, and by the following spring I was anxious to return to the harsh realities of the outside world.

Admiral di Giamberardino had gone, posted to a derisory command in Corsica where there were no conquered French for him to treat with compassion and understanding. Before he left he gave me a commendation praising my work for his delegation. Without actually saying so he indicated that he had misgivings about German intentions towards the French and he felt that an enthusiastic reference from the Officer Commanding the Armistice Commission would carry weight as long as Italy and Germany remained Axis partners.

His successor, also an admiral, was an ardent Fascist and the elegant rooms of the hotel sprouted pictures of the Duce. It was not the same at all, and I was thankful when Commandant Nomurat asked me to return to Nice and hold myself in readiness for the next mission, whenever it might be. My mother went ahead to find us somewhere to live and in the meantime we would stay at the Hotel Alsace-Lorraine. Having been there so often to meet Le Petit I had become very friendly with the proprietress, Madame Gauthier, and I thought this remarkable woman would be someone for Mummy to talk to when I was away. Also members of the Deuxième Bureau had to be even more circumspect about keeping rendezvous at the hotel than they had been before the defeat of France, and I would, paradoxically, be less conspicuous if I was actually living at the hotel than if I made frequent visits to it.

After ten months of living rent free and with food provided

my salary had built up quite nicely, and Mother's commission on her shopping for the Italians had made us comparatively affluent. I had no hesitation, therefore, in travelling first class from Toulon to Nice. In the carriage were two men speaking to each other in an Italian dialect which was unfamiliar to me. One of them looked very striking. He was only about five feet tall and his head was as bald as Koci's. But in spite of this he did not look ridiculous. His features were very clean cut and he gave the impression of pent-up energy. I guessed him to be in his early thirties. He reminded me very much of some of the better portraits of Napoleon – those which suggest dynamic power. It was the likeness to Napoleon which gave me a clue to the dialect – these men must be Corsicans.

One of them said something witty and the small one noticed that I smiled. Seeing that I understood Italian he spoke to me and we had an interesting conversation, talking of music and painting but never of the war. He expressed his views forcefully and concisely, a very clear-thinking man. When we approached Nice he asked me where in the city I lived.

'Number 3, rue Alsace-Lorraine,' I replied. There was no reason why I should not disclose that I was going to stay at Madame Gauthier's hotel but I was wary of mentioning it to a stranger. However he recognized the address because when we said good-bye he added, 'And please remember me to Madame Gauthier. My name is Simon Cotoni.'

I gave his message and Madame Gauthier nodded. 'He is in the police,' she told me, nothing more. Running a hotel which was a meeting place for secret agents required discretion and courage, both of which qualities Madame Gauthier possessed in abundance. However worrying things were she was always the same, imperturbable, courteous and immaculately dressed. She was one of the best groomed women I have ever seen and although her origins were *petit bourgeois* she had the poise and composure of a duchess.

We did not stay long at the Alsace-Lorraine because we were fortunate enough to find a flat which we loved. It really was very sweet, furnished in the Provençal style. Although it had only two little rooms besides a kitchen and bathroom it was quite charming and for the first time since leaving Vienna we felt that we had a home of our own. Erna and Hansi were living in Nice and they often came to see us or we would go to them. We also became friendly with a Colonel and Mrs Jacobson who had come to Nice from Paris when it was occupied by the Germans. Colonel Jacobson had been in the Foreign Legion and had lost an arm in the First World War, just four hours before the Armistice.

Still waiting for a new assignment, I had plenty of time on my hands and I was able to lead a normal life – or as normal as one could in defeated France in 1941. Nothing was being imported any more, and many of the things – such as coffee – which one had always taken for granted disappeared altogether. Other things could be bought only on the black market at prices which my mother and I could not possibly afford. But the rationing, the shortages, the deprivations could not, we told each other, go on for ever. One day Hitler would be defeated – if we had not been certain before, we recognized that he had sealed his own fate with his invasion of Russia. Many people, far better informed than we were, considered that the war was lost that long hot summer and within weeks the British and the Russians would cease to resist. But even when the Germans were within a hundred miles of Moscow and hammering on the doors of Stalingrad, and the British were retreating across the Western Desert, my mother and I never lost faith. Just be patient a little while longer, only a little while. In the meantime keep on living.

It was not until the end of August, four months after I left Hyères, that Commandant Nomurat summoned me to Toulon to brief me for my new mission.

The British, anticipating a German drive south-eastwards to the Persian oilfields, had advanced northwards from their Egyptian and Palestinian bases to occupy the Lebanon and Syria. There had been short sharp clashes with the French troops, who considered themselves bound in honour to resist. Now these troops, disarmed, were to be repatriated to France. There were, Nomurat told me, about two thousand of them and some horses. Arrangements had been made for the safe conduct of two ships to sail from Toulon to Beirut and back. First the *Massiglia* – the ship on which the Prime Minister Daladier had escaped at the time of the Fall of France – and when she returned the second ship, the *Colombie,* would take the same route. For the western half of the journey there would be an escort of Italian ships and in the eastern Mediterranean a British escort would take the ship into Beirut.

'I'm sending you as a sort of welfare officer. But what I really want you to do is photograph the Straits of Messina. It's a wonderful opportunity for finding out what the Italians are doing there.'

He gave me a telephoto lens for my Leica and, as an afterthought, enquired if I had ever been on a sea voyage before.

'No,' I said, 'I've only been on very short trips and I'm always seasick.'

He smiled, the patronizing smile of the professional sailor.

'Seasickness is just imagination.'

Good, fine, I thought to myself. If he says seasickness is imagination, well all right, I will just imagine I am not seasick.

'You'll be passing through the Straits about six o'clock on Monday morning. The light will be good at that time of day – before the heat haze gets going. You won't have time to change the film but spread the thirty-six pictures out as evenly as you can so that we get an idea of distances.'

He told me that also on the *Massiglia* would be a *Capitaine de frégate* by the name of Barjot who would be in charge of the embarkation of the troops. There would be no other naval officers or ratings on board.

After the months of inactivity it was wonderful to have a job to do. And the prospect of a trip to the Middle East was exciting – doubly so because I had never been there and it would provide a temporary escape from the cage which France had become.

I was delighted with my stateroom on the liner – mahogany panelling and its own freshwater bathroom. I had expected it to have a little round porthole but instead there was quite a big window, giving on to the deck. The bed had a lovely rubber mattress. What a pity the trip would take only ten days!

Capitaine Barjot turned out to be a short fat man. He seemed friendly and intelligent which was just as well because I would obviously be seeing a lot of him.

The *Massiglia* nosed her way out of Toulon harbour and headed out into the Mediterranean. I immediately felt sick.

It was all very well for Commandant Nomurat to call it imagination. It may have been, for him. For me it was ghastly reality. I tottered as far as my bed and there I remained. I could not eat. I could not sleep. I could not even be sick. I lay, inert and suffering, feeling that I was going to die and hoping it would be soon.

Barjot, taking an evening stroll round the deck, put his head in at the window to ask how I was. In a weak voice I asked him to come to my cabin as I had something important to ask him. When he was seated, bulging over the sides of the little armchair, I made my request, baldly and plainly. I was far too ill for any finesse.

'I have to photograph the Straits of Messina. It's an order, you see. You do understand don't you? You must help me.'

'What do you mean, help you?'

'First you've got to get me on to the bridge. I'm so weak – you'll almost have to carry me. Then you'll have to shield me. You see they've given me this great lens to put on my little camera. It's like an elephant's trunk sticking out.'

My voice was shaking with self-pity. Barjot nodded firmly.

'Certainly I'll help you.'

Next morning, exerting all my willpower and with Barjot half carrying me I finally stumbled on to the bridge. I summoned all my strength to hold the camera steady as I swung it left, right, left. The telescopic lens would, I hoped, reveal far more than the naked eye could see. If anybody on the escorting craft had happened to raise his binoculars and look in my direction he could have hardly failed to see what was going on, with Barjot dodging about to conceal me from view without obstructing the lens and me wildly waving the camera. But I was too ill to care.

What made it all the more difficult was that the *Massiglia* did not sail a straight course. The Straits were heavily mined and our escort jinked back and forth to show us the way.

At last I had finished the film. I clambered down to my cabin and lay on the bed wondering dully how long seasickness could last.

All day I lay there and that night I did at last sleep for a few hours. In the morning the seasickness had gone. The sea was calm, I was hungry and the world had started up again.

Later in the day I sought out Barjot. I was not surprised that he had helped me because we were both under naval orders.

But I had given myself away to him. There was no possible hope that he could for one moment have thought that in my condition I would have tottered up on the bridge to take happy snaps for my holiday album. If he chose to inform on me I would be treated as a traitor, an enemy spy.

I did not think he would inform on me. We were both in the French Navy and I was sure that he could never betray anybody in the same service as himself. But I had to know.

Very slowly and cautiously I sounded out his views. He was extremely discreet and gave nothing away. Without putting it into words he conveyed to me the impression that he would not welcome a German victory. With that I had to be content.

I had heard, before I left France, that there were no shortages in Beirut and I had scraped together three thousand francs – a whole month's pay – which I firmly intended to spend on food and cigarettes and perhaps a pair of shoes. But food and cigarettes anyway.

'If you think,' said Barjot, 'that the British will allow you ashore in Beirut you are sadly mistaken. I'm the only person who'll be allowed to land – and that's only because I have to superintend the repatriation of the troops.'

This was a grave disappointment.

'Oh dear,' I said. 'That is a blow. But never mind. You can do my shopping for me. Cigarettes, of course. And sardines, I believe you can get sardines, coffee of course and . . .'

Barjot sighed. 'I shall be in uniform,' he said.

'But of course. What about it?'

'Do you really imagine that a French officer *in uniform* would be seen *carrying parcels* through the streets of Beirut?'

Years later I read in a newspaper that General de Gaulle, when attending President Kennedy's funeral, asked to see President Johnson. He was told that the President would naturally be delighted to see him but that many other heads of state had made the same request. He would, therefore, have to take his place in the queue. The newspaper reported the General as saying 'the President of France does not stand in a queue'. When I read that, all these years later, I was reminded of the tone of voice Barjot used when I asked him to shop for me.

'No, of course not. Silly of me,' I muttered, chastened.

'Never mind,' he said kindly. 'I shall be buying provisions for the troops and the crew of the ship. I'll see you get your share of the rations. That I promise you.'

Then, after a pause, he said quietly.

'I think – mind you I'm only guessing – that the British would probably relax the rule about leaving the ship for anybody who wanted to join de Gaulle. Do *you* want to join de Gaulle?'

'No. No. I must go back.'

He nodded and changed the subject.

Barjot had guessed right. As soon as the gangway was in position and the Australian soldiers had taken up their guard duties the exodus from the ship began. It seemed to me that half the crew, carrying their belongings and laughing and joking as they waved good-bye, tripped down the gangway. Wistfully I watched them go. It did not occur to me to take the opportunity of going myself to join the Free French – my duty was to work within France. But I dearly wanted to go ashore in Beirut.

At the head of the gangway stood the English army captain in command of the soldiers. As he watched the crew disembarking he was tapping his thigh with his short leather-covered swagger stick. I tried to catch his eye.

I have always found that if you look at someone hard enough they will eventually become aware of it, and when the captain looked at me I smiled and strolled towards him.

'I've got some information which might interest your people,' I murmured as I passed.

'Who are you?' he asked in French.

'Officially I'm a welfare assistant.'

The lips beneath the moustache twitched with amusement and the captain beckoned to a subaltern. 'Please take this lady to my office.' It was a relief to find that the captain was a man who could instantly make up his mind.

I realized that leaving the ship, even talking to the Englishman, was a dangerous thing to do. The ship's officers could hardly fail to notice and it would be very awkward for me if they should report the incident.

I was taken to a big wooden shed where the captain soon joined me.

'I can't leave the harbour for a couple of hours yet,' he

told me. 'But wouldn't you like to see the town in the mean-time?'

It was too good to be true. Yet it was true. I set off on my glorious shopping expedition in a Royal Navy car with a driver who knew exactly where things could be bought. First we loaded up with cartons of cigarettes – oh so cheap! There was a queue of soldiers and they were talking German. For a moment I thought I must be imagining it, but then I saw they were Czechs. It was a thrill to exchange a few words with my countrymen, all of us so far from home, before I dashed off in search of the next item on my shopping list. Tins of this, tins of that, coffee, coffee, coffee, sardines. An abundance of all things I had not seen for two years.

When the car was full and my purse empty we started back to the harbour. On the way a traffic policeman held us up at a crossroads and another car drew up alongside. Glancing idly at it I was overjoyed to see that it contained Barjot. I tapped on the window and he looked round. Inclining my head I smiled and gestured at the packages piled on the back seat.

The policeman waved us on and the driver let in the clutch. But as we moved away I was able to see Barjot's expression of amazement and consternation.

The captain was waiting when we got back to the office in the harbour. He asked my name and told me his – Geoffrey Household.

'And what is this interesting information?' he asked.

'Well actually it's not really what you'd call *information*. But I took some photographs coming through the Straits of Messina. Would they be of interest?'

'Yes. Yes, I should think they might. It's practically impossible to do any aerial reconnaissance there nowadays.'

'I can't give you this film because I've got to take it back. But I shall be coming back on the *Colombie* when she comes to take home some more prisoners.'

'Not prisoners,' Captain Household broke in. 'The Vichy troops are being evacuated with the Honours of War in eight-eenth-century style.'

'Well anyhow. Shall I take another film for you?'

'Please do. And I'll arrange for an Intelligence officer to have a word with you.'

'If you can't take any aerial photographs perhaps you don't know that you have hit the *Bolzano*. Barjot told me he saw her in Messina. He was looking through his binoculars.'

Captain Household nodded but whether or not the information was new to him I had no way of telling.

'Would you like a chart of the way we came through the minefield?' I asked.

At last I succeeded in arousing his interest and his response was eager.

'Of course I'm not a sailor,' I told him. 'But I think if you ask him – tactfully you understand – Barjot might give it to you.'

Barjot was waiting for me when I returned to the ship with my booty. When he asked me how I had managed to get ashore I looked hard at him.

'I told them I had some information for them. I hadn't, as a matter of fact. But, you know, I gather from your manner that you would prefer the Allies to win the war.'

He did not respond. But at least he did not deny it.

'Give it a thought,' I said. 'Don't you think you should do something about it if you can?'

'I am a French officer,' he replied stiffly. 'My honour would not permit . . .'

'That of course is a matter for your own mind and your own heart. Yet don't you agree, sometimes it's better to do the wrong thing than nothing at all?'

We talked in this vein for several hours. I told Barjot that the British wanted a chart of the Messina minefields. He was non-committal. I left the subject alone and returned to it a little later. Finally he said, 'Well, I suppose there's no harm in giving it to them. I mean it's nothing to do with France.'

I do not suggest that it was I who convinced Barjot that he could best serve France by serving the Allies. It was entirely his own decision. Men of his calibre make up their own minds. But perhaps those long hours of discussion helped him to clarify his thoughts, to question where his true loyalties should lie.

When, at last, he promised to give the chart of the minefields to Captain Household the next day I turned to more mundane matters and borrowed some money from him to go shopping.

After I had bought a pair of shoes – being a secret agent

is exceedingly hard on the feet I had discovered – I went into a chemist's shop.

'Isn't there anything you can take to prevent seasickness? Anything at all? Surely there must be something?'

The chemist seemed surprised. 'But of course.'

He gave me some pills and for the whole of the voyage back I never felt ill once. When I went to report to Commandant Nomurat I told him triumphantly that I had found this marvellous cure.

'And on the voyage out I just lay on my bed and thought how wrong you were to tell me that seasickness is imagination.'

'If your seasickness wasn't imagination the cure certainly was.'

I just had time to deliver parcels of lovely food and cigarettes to all my friends in Nice before it was time to go back to Toulon to board the second ship, the *Colombie*. Colonel Jacobson had provided finance for another shopping spree, I had great faith in the Arab chemist's pills and I was looking forward to the trip.

This time, as we left the harbour, the alarm rang for a practice alert and we all proceeded to boat stations. I remarked to Barjot that I was surprised that it should be necessary because the belligerents had been informed of the voyage of this unarmed neutral ship but he explained that it was routine. Apparently there had been boat drill on the *Massiglia* as well but I had been far too ill to notice.

A few days later the alarm sounded again. It was a very hot afternoon and I was sitting in my cabin wearing a nightdress and painting my toenails. I decided to take no notice. After a few minutes the sound of the bells and of running feet died away. I stuffed lumps of cotton wool between my toes and started to paint the nails of the other foot. The ship was quiet now but I could hear aircraft droning overhead. There was a bang on the door.

'Who's there?'

'Come on. Boat stations. Hurry.' Barjot's voice.

'Oh I can't. I'm so busy. Let me pretend I haven't heard.'

'*Come on*. It's real.'

'That's different. I'm coming.'

Instinctively I grabbed my Leica. I did not have to think

what was my most important possession. I picked up the camera with no more hesitation than Mother, in similar circumstances, would have picked up Dougo.

With the paint wet on my toenails I could not put on shoes even if there had been time. So, holding the hem of my nightdress clear of the varnish and mincing along with the cotton wool between my toes, I made my way to my boat station escorted by a highly embarrassed Barjot.

I soon forgot the wolf whistles of the crew when the bombing began. As the individual planes peeled off and began their bomb runs we could see the markings on their wings.

'Italian bastards!' shouted the crew. 'Macaronis!'

Without even a single anti-aircraft gun the *Colombie* wallowed helplessly at the mercy of the bombs dropping like eggs from the belly of the leading plane. My first experience of bombing – I was too excited, indignant, too angry, to be frightened, too fascinated by sunlight glinting silver on the bombs.

To raise the camera was a reflex action. I did it without reasoning, not pausing to think why I should.

Plumes of water rose like fountains. The *Colombie* twisted and turned like a hunted stag seeking to evade its tormenting hounds. The planes turned and started a second run. Again the bombs fell wide.

I braced myself for the third attempt. It did not come. The planes flew off and I watched them until they were out of sight. Then I went back to my cabin and finished painting my toenails.

Again Barjot tapped on the door.

'Let me have your film, will you? We can use it as evidence when we make our official complaint.'

Geoffrey Household was standing at the top of the gangway. We had agreed not to let prying eyes aboard the *Colombie* see that we knew one another. His nod was almost imperceptible and he waggled his eyebrow to indicate the car standing on the quay. I glanced round quickly and chose a moment when I thought no one was watching to slip down the gangway and into the waiting car. At the wheel was a young man, fair-haired and blue-eyed. Not the one who had driven me on my shopping expedition last time. He chatted easily and amusingly in excellent French as he drove me to a restaurant at the foot of the mountains behind Beirut.

Rather to my surprise he did not wait for his officer but took me straight in to lunch. I was puzzled and a little annoyed. I wanted to hand over the film and get on with my shopping. Also, I must confess, I thought that I was being treated too casually. I, a member of the clandestine Deuxième Bureau, had come all the way from the far end of the Mediterranean and the best these British could do was to send a driver to take me out to lunch. An amusing and agreeable companion, certainly, but I really did think I deserved the attention of somebody more important.

'I hope your officer will be coming soon,' I said. 'This is very pleasant but I have work to do, you know.'

'My officer?' He looked blankly at me.

'Yes. I understood from Captain Household that I was going to meet an officer in your Intelligence.'

A grin replaced the blank look.

'Oh. Oh, I do beg your pardon. I should have introduced myself. I'm the chap you're supposed to see. Geoffrey Household told me it might be worth having a word with you. By the way, my name's William Astor.'

I choked and hastily took a gulp of water.

'Are you related to Lord Astor?'

'My father.'

There are three or four names, such as Rothschild, which are known all over the world. Astor is one of them. Since early childhood I had heard of the Astors.

'And your mother – she is a Deputy in your English House of Representatives?'

The grin broadened.

'Well, yes. Actually we call it a Member of Parliament.'

I had absent-mindedly picked up a hard-boiled egg and bitten into it. Mummy would have been furious. I hastily put it back on my plate and took a knife and fork.

I handed over my film. In response to a delicately phrased enquiry I said that I did not want to leave France and join de Gaulle. William Astor did not pursue the point. He was much more gentle, much softer than I expected an Intelligence officer to be. Dino, or even Le Petit would have subjected me to a harsh cross-examination. I had met few Englishmen. I did not recognize under-statement when I met it. Nor had I ever heard of that uniquely British phenomenon, the talented amateur.

'I do hope,' said William Astor, 'that when this silly war is over you'll come to London. Do look me up. 45 Upper Grosvenor Street. And if there's anything I can do in the meantime . . .'

'In the meantime there is nothing. But after the war is over . . .

'Yes?'

I am teetotal and had been drinking only water. But I was intoxicated.

'I would like to have dinner with Winston Churchill.'

William Astor looked at me gravely. Then, quietly, he said, 'That can be arranged.'

Chapter 13

I suppose that the photographs of the Messina Straits would in any case have reached the British. Obviously Commandant Nomurat did not want his set of pictures for his own enjoyment – they would be sent by undercover routes to the Allied Command presumably, though I had no proof of this, through Algiers and to the Free French. But it was a great satisfaction to me to know that I had given one set of the pictures directly to the only country which was fighting the Axis powers in the Mediterranean.

On the return voyage I had many long talks with Barjot. It was fascinating to watch a man of the highest intelligence and the highest honour who was not sure – undoubtedly for the first and probably for the only time in his life – what were the dictates of his conscience.

In conquered France there were many who had similar traumas. But in the little coterie to which I belonged in Nice we all felt that we were more useful remaining in France than escaping to join de Gaulle. We were not soldiers – either, like me, we were unsuited or, like Le Petit, the jobs we were doing clandestinely were far more useful than any overt action we could perform in the Free French forces.

I soon realized that Colonel Jacobson, the one-armed ex-Legionnaire, was engaged in some undercover activity or other, and one day I met Simon Cotoni in the street.

'Don't know me. Keep walking, keep walking,' he said without moving his lips. With me marching in front, concentrating on not looking round, we conducted a short exchange of news – nothing important but it gave me a sense of hope. I realized that France was not dead. People like Cotoni, Le Petit, and Jacobson were using their brains and their courage to carry on the fight against Hitler. I was proud to be accepted by, and numbered among, such men.

At this time we were recruiting agents so that we could pass on a complete picture of the Italian coast as far as Genoa. But some of them were of a very different type from those who had been enrolled when our organization had been the official Intelligence Service of the French Navy. Now we were finding certain of our agents among poachers and petty criminals, smugglers who lived on the French side of the frontier and who constantly made sorties across into Italy.

It was through my old friend Ailhaud that we had a ready supply. He would carefully screen all men charged with offences to do with the frontier and delicately suggest to suitable ones that if they cared to co-operate in the passing of information the charges could be dropped. He was very good at summing them up, and all the men he recommended to us were intelligent and courageous. Oddly enough they turned out to be more reliable than the agents who had been employed previously. The life they had been living on the fringes of society had sapped any self-respect they may have had but now all that was changed. With a task which they could see was worthwhile and lavish praise when they did it well they suddenly found a purpose.

A good agent must have ideals. Money, though an important incentive, was not enough to buy their services. There must be an inner compulsion, loyalty to a cause. That is the foundation without which an agent cannot be built.

Spying is a strange business, the way in which it grips those engaged in it. It is like getting hooked on a drug. The commitment becomes total, the dedication complete.

These poachers and smugglers of ours could move freely in the secret places of the Alps with utter confidence – they had known how to evade the frontier posts all their lives. And in Italy itself they aroused no suspicion. They were of the frontier region, they spoke its dialect, there was nothing about them to indicate that they had been born on the west rather than the east side of the imaginary line which divided people, who lived a few yards from each other, into Frenchmen and Italians. The risk of being stopped by the Italian police and asked for their papers was slight. The police had no reason to stop poorly-dressed workmen, walking or cycling. And if they had, our men would simply say that they had left their papers at home and offer to go and get them. Then of course they would have nipped back over the frontier out of harm's way.

With a countryman's eye each one was a natural observer and they brought accurate reports of fortifications, of ships, of troop movements. We instilled into them the importance of punctuality. Lateness is a danger signal and any espionage organization reacts energetically to it, in self-preservation. We could not afford false alarms.

I was often given the job of interviewing these men when they came to report. On grounds of security we did not want them to know any one of us well enough to give a description if they should be caught and interrogated, and it is much easier for a woman to disguise herself than a man. All I had to do was to leave off my make-up, put on a large pair of sun glasses and tie a headscarf carefully to hide my hair. I became anonymous, unidentifiable.

We had to limit our coverage to Genoa because that was about as far as these men could go on bicycles. We dared not let them travel by train because the police often checked papers on trains and it would have been unnatural as well as illegal to travel without them. There was, of course, no question of using cars. There was no petrol, these men did not possess cars, and in any case they would not have been able to get a car across the frontier.

Another frontier had recently sprung up – that between the Zone which the Germans occupied and the so-called 'Free Zone'. Only those who could show good reason to travel were given permits to cross it and it was always interesting to meet such people and hear what conditions were like in Paris and the area where the German presence was most strongly felt. One evening I met a man from Paris at the Jacobsons'. His name was Taudu and he had called to see his old friends – both he and Colonel Jacobson were freemasons – on his way back from Toulon where he had been on business.

He walked home with me and began paying me compliments. I found this irritating. He was an ugly man with a head too big for his body, badly dressed, and his compliments were flowery in the extreme. If he had been handsome and elegant he might have sounded sincere but to me he seemed ridiculous. I quickened my pace.

Did I, he enquired, have a boy-friend? Nothing special, I told him.

'I had a very unfortunate experience last year,' I said. 'I fell in love with an Italian but then Italy declared war and so now we're enemies. That's that, finished.'

I thought of Dino, strong as an oak tree, and I looked at this figure shambling along paying me high-flown compliments. To stop them I had to say something so I asked him what he did for a living.

'I have a factory which makes ropes and cables – *La Corderie du Nord.*'

Then he asked me if there was anything I would like him to send me. Ropes and cables were of no interest to me, I explained. But no, no, he had not meant to send me anything from the factory. Was there, perhaps, something I would like from the farm? Yes there was. Potatoes.

'Potatoes?'

'Potatoes.'

I thought no more about it but three weeks later a large sack arrived containing not only potatoes but many things, such as tins of *pâté de foie gras* which were unheard-of luxuries. There was very strict rationing but there was no guarantee that the rations would be met and often they were not. We and our closest friends would often have gone hungry if it had not been for the tins I had brought back from Beirut. The sack from Taudu was, therefore, a welcome gift.

With it was a letter. He had, it said, fallen so much under my spell that he hoped he might see me again. He had a great deal he wanted to tell me. He asked if I would meet him in Cannes. He would, he said, book two rooms at the Grand Hotel for us. There would be no strings attached, no obligation on me except a request to listen to what he had to say.

'What a charming man he must be,' Mummy exclaimed.

'Do you think I ought to go to Cannes?'

'Oh yes, why not? He is obviously very fond of you or he wouldn't have sent such a lovely parcel. The Grand, I'm told, is a splendid hotel. Yes, go. You'll enjoy it. You see, he says here there won't be any strings attached.' She paused. 'And even if there are,' she added, 'what have you got to lose?'

He arranged to be there first and would meet me at the station.

I set off with a certain excitement, venturing into the unknown. I had forgotten quite what he looked like. In my imagination he had become much more handsome, much more elegant, much more this, much more that.

The sight of him brought me back to earth with a bump.

'Ah,' he said, clasping his hands. 'So you have arrived!'

I nearly turned round there and then and went straight back to Nice. I love to be loved but this was adoration. It was like being bathed in honey, sweet and sticky. I thought of Dino, so strong, Dino with his clear direct speech. So different from this humble supplicant.

Mother had been right about the Grand Hotel. The rooms were magnificent. I had never been in a hotel like this before. The elegance took my breath away – thick carpets, and chandeliers, and waiters with white gloves moving swiftly and silently carrying silver trays. It was like the Hotel Châteaubriand all over again but with one enormous difference. The Châteaubriand had been taken over by the Armistice Commission and I was an employee. Here was a hotel being used for its proper purpose and I was a guest. At the Châteaubriand Admiral di Giamberardino had made me pretend to be a countess. Here there was no pretence. At the Châteaubriand I had been Cinderella waiting for twelve o'clock. Here twelve o'clock would never strike. I, the little refugee from Vienna, was here in my own right, determined to enjoy every minute of it.

The lunch cost two thousand francs – two thirds of a month's pay for me. But, sadly it was wasted on me. I had never eaten oysters before and the idea of swallowing those slimy greyish things which shrivelled when I put lemon juice on them revolted me. I was not encouraged when Taudu explained that they were alive.

He was very patient. The treat which he had planned had misfired but he remained as considerate and concerned as ever. I hid my dismay as best I could, out of politeness – and felt the beginnings of affection for a man who could go to so much trouble on my behalf.

153

As we strolled on the Croisette he quoted poetry. I like poetry when I am in the mood for it. I was not, and I thought it mushy.

Dinner was an ordeal. I found myself refusing nearly everything he suggested. I am sorry, I do not drink champagne. I do not drink anything except water. No, really I do not. No oysters, I beg you. I never want to see another oyster. No, I am afraid I did not like the caviar much. I am not used to caviar.

It was an exhausting day and I was thankful to go to bed. I half expected he would suggest coming to my room but he did not. At least, I thought, I am spared having to say no yet again.

Next morning he talked more sensibly. He was knowledgeable and interesting about politics and the war situation. He had fought in the 1914 war and, at forty-one, had been just too old to rejoin his regiment in 1939. But he was as strongly anti-Hitler as I was myself. I was surprised to find that the morning had passed quite quickly.

But after lunch – he had an aperitif, white wine, red wine, brandy, while I drank water – he became sentimental again. By the evening he was getting badly on my nerves. All the shrewdness and wisdom of the morning had gone. Taudu was a dreamer and I did not know where I was with him. All these protestations of love – did he mean them or not? I had no idea. Fact and fantasy were so inextricably mixed up.

In the evening we went to the Casino and down to the restaurant – the Brummell – which was candle-lit and romantic with a Czech violinist playing haunting music. Taudu was at his most poetic, his most sentimental. I yawned behind my hand.

'You do dislike me, don't you?' The directness of the question was a relief from the cocoons of silky words.

'No, I wouldn't say I dislike you exactly. In fact in some ways I find you interesting.'

'Then perhaps you would like to know more?'

'Frankly, no.'

'Why not?'

'Because you are so saturating.'

'How can anybody,' he exclaimed, 'be so brutally sincere!'

'Well I'm sorry but it's true. All this poetry – all these flowery compliments.'

'Does it matter?'

'It does to me.'

'I suppose I disgust you physically too?'

'You neither disgust nor attract me. You see, Monsieur Taudu' (I had not bothered to ask his Christian name) 'with me it's mental companionship which comes first. Sex works downwards not upwards.'

We went back to the hotel soon afterwards, to our separate bedrooms.

Next day was much the same except that I found that his intellect had wider horizons than I had at first thought. The previous day I had been impressed by his shrewdness. Now other things began to show themselves. I realized that this was a man who – with all his superficially unattractive habits – had a breadth of vision far greater than I had imagined. He was an uncharted country, stretching into infinity. It would take a lifetime to explore it. But I had no wish to begin.

Again we went to the Brummell. Again the Czech violinist played haunting music. Again I refused champagne.

That night Taudu asked to come to my room. Only to talk. I said I would meet him in the sitting room between our bedrooms.

He knelt on the floor at my feet, tears running down his cheeks.

'You're like a crocodile who cries while he devours his prey. I shall call you Croco.'

We went to bed.

We spent three more days together. He stopped the fulsome compliments, so he was no longer irritating. But we did not draw mentally closer.

'I hope that one day you will come to love me,' he said. I just shrugged my shoulders.

All the same, when he had gone back to Paris and I to Nice I missed him. Or perhaps I missed the luxury of the Grand Hotel. For the first time since my father died I had not even been conscious of having to economize, to be careful over money. To live, if only for a week, the life of a princess, and not of a refugee.

I told myself that many refugees were worse off than me, as indeed they were. Jews who had fled from Germany and the German occupied countries and found a temporary haven were now at risk. The Italians were not anti-Semitic but they followed the official Axis policy and surrendered to the Nazis any Jews not protected by Italian or neutral nationality. Our own agents helped many of them to escape, guiding them over the secret passes and paths through the mountains and being paid handsomely for it.

The German grip tightened on France all through the summer of 1942. The Germans still thought they would win the war but it was taking longer than they had expected and they no longer cared what the French thought of them. The Jewish refugees knew that they would not be safe for long.

Those who could afford to, paid huge sums to be smuggled into Spain. Those who could not, sat and waited for Fate to overtake them.

Then the Germans demanded that all Jews holding German passports should be handed over by the French authorities. The French prevaricated and procrastinated as much as they could but they could not refuse. German citizens were German citizens.

My mother met many Jews among the refugees who gathered at the Casino, trying to live a hollow echo of a social life. She did what she could for these piteous people and when the whispers came 'the hunt for the Jews is on' we sheltered them for the night of fear. But there were many nights of fear.

Once we had twenty-two frightened people in our flat – but we were only postponing the inevitable. Trains with cattle-trucks crammed with humanity trundled remorselessly to the concentration camps. The fortunate ones died on the journey.

The horrors were so overwhelming that one did not dare to stop and contemplate them. Otherwise one would oneself have died of despair.

I thanked God that I had work to do. That I could contribute something, however little, to the overthrow of Nazi evil. I plunged ever more whole-heartedly into whatever task I was given.

One day Le Petit came to see me, his expression downcast. Oddly unlike himself, normally so eager and confident, he was deeply embarrassed. I had to ask him outright why he had come before he could bring himself to the point.

'I don't really know how to begin,' he said unhappily. 'You see, it's all because Cotoni has tipped us off that the Alsace-Lorraine isn't safe any more.'

'Cotoni?'

'Yes. He's warned us to be careful. He thinks the Italians know about the hotel.'

This was grave news.

'But Madame Gauthier? Are they on to her?'

'Probably. But they can't do anything. Under the terms of the Armistice they can't arrest a French citizen. If they've got a charge against one they're obliged to ask the French police to make the arrest. And, you can imagine, Cotoni would see that she was warned if the Italians wanted her arrested. Oh, don't worry. Madame Gauthier isn't in any danger.

'But we're not to use her hotel any more?'

'Exactly. And that's why I'm here. I've come to ask if you will let one of the agents – a girl – come to your flat. She'll need to spend a night once a fortnight or so.'

'But of course. No problem.'

'Ah well, it's not as simple as that. There is a problem – a moral problem.'

'A moral problem? Am I involved?'

He gulped. 'Well yes. Partly. You see, this girl . . . Well, she's a prostitute.'

He looked pleadingly at me.

'I mean I know it's a terrible thing to ask. And of course you can't decide without talking it over with your mother.'

'Tell me more about her.'

'She's Austrian. She's got a child. One of our agents found her in a brothel in Genoa.'

'But what's a brothel got to do with espionage?'

'It's a cheap brothel, apparently. Sailors go there. German and Italian naval ratings. And merchant seamen. She can find out their ships – it would be very valuable information for us. After all, she sees about twenty men a day.'

'Twenty a day!'

Le Petit nodded miserably.

I did, as he suggested, consult my mother. We came to the

conclusion that we had no alternative but to agree. We thought of the Jews we had sheltered, hustled away to their deaths. Our sacrifice would be a very small one.

'Your mother,' Le Petit remarked when I told him we would have the girl, 'could perhaps be a little kind to her. And you could tell her some of the things you've learned yourself.'

Mummy rose to the occasion. The girl was called Marlene, and she treated her exactly as she used to treat the friends I brought home from school. The girl was pitifully grateful. She was shy and unsure of herself, very conscious of her shame. Her story was not unusual. An illegitimate child. A social outcast. In the city of Vienna there were two million inhabitants and half a million out of work, before the Nazis marched in. (Dictatorships thrive on the unemployed.) Marlene tried her luck in Italy. Same story. She drifted into a brothel. That was that.

On her fortnightly visits she really did bring us valuable information. She was paid well for her information and the money made it easy for her to pay for the fostering of her child. She became more relaxed. Mummy's genius for home-making made her feel accepted. Lustre returned to the huge brown eyes. Life started again for her.

Croco Taudu wrote. He was coming again to the Free Zone. Would I meet him in Cannes? This time we went to a different hotel – the Carlton. These very luxurious hotels were having a hard job to keep going at all and they had not raised their prices to the level of the roaring inflation. (I had considerable sympathy with them because my own salary was still at the pre-war rate!) Consequently a gorgeous suite of sitting room, two huge bedrooms and two bathrooms cost about half the price of dinner in the restaurant.

With the insincerity and the nonsense removed, Taudu showed his real qualities. He was clever, he was generous and he was considerate. I managed to forget that he was ugly. Colonel Jacobson had told me that Taudu had had an unhappy life. His father had been an alcoholic, his first wife had committed suicide, his present wife had left him.

It was one evening at the Brummell where we had gone to hear the Czech violinist play that Taudu told me about his first wife. She had been Polish, a ballet dancer, and he married her when she was seventeen. One day he returned home to find she had gone. Hours later the police came to tell him that she had been found dead, shot with Taudu's old army revolver which she had taken from a drawer in his desk. She was twenty-one.

That was six years ago and Taudu, I think, loved her still. I reminded him of her.

One day he made a suggestion. If I would take an unfurnished flat where he could come and stay he would give me a sum of money to decorate and equip it. It was a wonderful offer. Mummy and I were overjoyed.

We soon found a perfect flat. It was in the rue Rossini, on the fifth floor, but there was a small lift, slow and erratic, so we were able to take beds and chairs up there. It was almost impossible to get anything done – finding a replacement for a rusty lavatory chain was a major undertaking – but Taudu sent us paint from his factory and we haunted the second-hand shops.

Mother had not been so happy since we left Vienna. At last we were going to have a home of our own, and everything in it would be ours, chosen by ourselves. Her cup was full when she came back one afternoon gasping and out of breath, a large marble clock clasped under one arm and Dougo tugging at his lead. She proudly placed the clock on the mantelshelf in the sitting room, and stood back and looked at it. For her it was a symbol – the symbol of a new home, a fresh chapter.

In another way, too, the flat would make a big difference to our lives. Its rent was only half what we had been paying for the furnished one so we would be much better off. We would even be able to entertain our friends in a modest way. It might, in fact, be a help to Colonel Jacobson if I could take over some of the clandestine meetings. His flat in the Promenade des Anglais was on the ground floor, rather too open to the public gaze. Also he was careful to keep the details of his underground activities from his wife so that if he should be caught she would not be involved. In the same way I told Mummy only what it was essential for her to know. I had visions of her and Mrs Jacobson spending evenings together in one or other of the flats while Colonel Jacobson and I conferred with people of like mind in the other. We were already beginning to hear, filtering through from the Occupied Zone, reports of the formation of a Resistance movement and Colonel Jacobson was in touch with its representatives.

But before all these meetings could take place in our new flat we would have to move in ourselves. We redoubled our efforts to get it finished, exulting over every find we made – a carpet was a great event, a blanket was a red letter day.

In spite of the gathering clouds that summer was full of hope and interest. Taudu's visits when we stayed in a luxury hotel in Cannes – always a different one, the Grand, the Carlton, the Martinez – were something to look forward to, as was the flat itself. My work was becoming more and more rewarding with the agents proving reliable and informative. Marlene, the girl from the brothel in Genoa, was producing a mass of valuable intelligence. She would work for three weeks without taking her days off, saving them up so that she could make the trip to Nice to report. As she had a German passport she could come and go as she wished. She was resident in Italy so there was no difficulty in returning there and no French official would have dared to obstruct the free passage of one of the conquering race.

The most difficult thing was to instil in her a sense of confidence.

'I had a narrow escape yesterday,' she told me, on one of her early visits. 'I asked a customer the name of his ship and he said "Why do you want to know. Are you a spy?" It was terrible. I didn't know what to say.'

'What you should have said,' I told her, 'was "Of course I'm a spy. Why else would I be working in a brothel? You don't think I'm really a prostitute do you?" ' I went on to tell her that this was the method I had adopted in Sicily when the Italian Air Force officer had asked me the same question. 'He didn't believe me – he knew that if it had been true I would never have admitted it.'

I tried to teach her the technique I had evolved myself, of diverting attention away from the subject as soon as I had got the answer to my question.

'Look, suppose I was in your position. I would say to a man "What is the name of the captain of your ship?" He would ask me why I wanted to know and I would say, "Because there was a captain here a month ago and he gave me a nice present and said he'd come next time he was in port. His name was So-and-so. Is your captain So-and-so?" Then he would say, "No, our captain is called Such-and-such." Immediately I had the answer

I would switch to something else. "Oh I'm hungry! Do get me a sandwich. No, not a sandwich, I think I'd like an ice-cream." Get him thinking about something quite different, pretend to be hardly listening when he answers your question. Get him confused trying to follow every time you change your mind – sandwich to ice-cream, back to sandwich again.'

It was hard going at first but gradually I managed to stiffen her – to make her dominate the conversation in the last ten minutes of her customer's time with her.

By now we were all confident that our information was getting through to the Allies. We did not pry into the secrets of other undercover organizations but we were hearing more and more about the Free French and from the Occupied Zone came an increasing number of stories of how worried the Germans were getting about the mounting activities of the Resistance. It became a golden rule never to ask about the source of any news – in the event of our being caught the less we knew the better. However determined one might be one could never guarantee that one would not crack under Gestapo torture.

Le Petit brought me an item of news which made me proud.

'Your friend Barjot got through all right. He's with General de Gaulle in London now.'

Chapter 14

Taudu loved the flat. He was astonished at the way we had found workmen to do the decoration and alterations, at the way my mother had waved her wand and a home had sprung into being.

The war was now approaching that stage which Churchill later described as being 'not the beginning of the end, but the end of the beginning'. The pendulum had started its swing away from the Axis victories. I was surprised, therefore, at the doleful expression on Le Petit's face when he came one day to the flat. It was soon apparent that he had come to tell me something that I was not going to like. The question of Dino Castellani, he told me, had come up again. It was now obvious that our organization had direct contact with the Allies and the money could be made available to pay Dino to defect and to bring with him the Italian Naval Code. I was required to brief Marlene who could, without risk, approach Dino, going first to see his mother in Florence. Dino had, I knew, told his mother about me.

This was not at all to my liking. At first I had been a pawn in the international chess game. Now, it seemed, I was to be cast for the role of queen.

It was two and a half years since that brief, fierce affair in Venice. Two and a half eventful years in which I had changed, matured. By an effort of will I had put Dino out of my mind. Now I had Croco Taudu. He was my rock, and compared with his wisdom and kindness, his gentle strength, Dino's forcefulness seemed ruthless and brutal. I did not want to see Dino again.

I expected the timid and shy Marlene to be appalled at the prospect of seeking out the head of OVRA. But I had not reckoned with the characteristic which had drawn her to be a prostitute. She might not like men but she unquestionably understood them. She could handle Dino, of that she was confident. She nodded briskly. She was on her own ground.

'He's a remarkably attractive man,' I told her. 'He has a sort of magnetism.' She smiled wearily at my *naïveté*. She was a professional. She had seen it all before.

'Of course,' I said. 'He's probably forgotten about me. I don't for a moment expect that he'll come.' Although I was speaking to Marlene I was trying to convince myself.

'Don't you believe it,' she said cheerfully. 'Isn't he at what they call the dangerous age? When men throw up everything for the sake of a young girl?'

I was not comforted.

'Now for heaven's sake be careful what you say. Only speak about important things when you're in the open air and you can't be overheard.'

So Marlene set off to put the clock back two and a half years.

I expected it would take her three or four weeks even to arrange an appointment with Dino and I just had to live through the interval. Taudu was in Paris, the flat was furnished, I had nothing to do but wait.

Marlene turned up after only six days.

Yes, she had seen Dino. No, he wouldn't come. He still thought Germany and Italy would win the war. He would not defect.

My reaction to the news that I had not, after all, pulled off the greatest espionage coup of all time, was one of unalloyed relief. The relief was so great that I closed my eyes and almost fainted.

'Did you hear what I said?' Marlene asked.

'No. What?'

'He spoke very highly of you. And very tenderly. He sent you a message.' She paused.

'Yes?' I prompted.

'You have been condemned to death. In Rome, for espionage. You must be very careful. He thinks you ought to leave Nice. And, by the way, you were quite right. He's terribly sexy.' From a prostitute this was high praise, a considered professional opinion.

Neither Le Petit nor I took the condemnation in Rome very seriously. Italian histrionics, we considered it. But we were already uncomfortably aware that the OVRA knew too much about all of us – we had discovered that the Hotel Alsace-Lorraine had been under observation for a long time. It was not difficult for the OVRA to trace people who frequented it, and from them to get a lead on others. Colonel Jacobson's ground floor flat on the Promenade des Anglais was only too easy to watch.

On 6 November Taudu arrived to stay for a fortnight – the longest single visit he had made since I had known him. It was a lovely holiday. We were happy in our little home, Taudu, Mummy, Dougo and I. A family.

As a child I had loved my father unquestioningly, uncritically. But when I was twelve years old he fell ill and from then on he changed. He became irritable and unreasonable. I did not understand then that this change was due to physical reasons and I was deeply hurt by it.

It had the effect of making me self-reliant. I would have to look after myself – and my mother too. I was on my own with nowhere to run for shelter. It would, perhaps, have been easier if I had never experienced the emotional security of my father's love. Then I would not have realized what I had lost, and yearned for it.

Now Taudu was proving to be a father-figure. In him I recognized the paternal outlook which I had not found since the age of twelve. Always I think of emotional security in terms of being wrapped up – a soft fur coat, a fluffy blanket. Taudu was all-enveloping.

In spite of the bright sunshine there can be a chilly wind on the Riviera in autumn and several times Taudu took off his coat and slipped it over my shoulders – 'my little girl mustn't catch cold'. It was this sort of consideration which Dino would never have shown. He would have marched on, heedless of whether I could keep up with his long strides.

Looking back on my relationship with Dino I came to the conclusion that I had been very naïve. In my amateurish way I could never really have outwitted his high professionalism. He must have known all the time that I was a French agent. With the benefit of hindsight I could see why he had kept up the pretence. He had presumably come to Koci's little hotel primed with my dossier from Sicily and Genoa. Whether he had always intended to use me as a go-between I could not tell. Nor had I any way of discovering whether it was before or after meeting me that he determined to defect to France. If he had come to Venice with the intention of getting in touch with the Deuxième Bureau through that Bureau's agent there, he had certainly succeeded.

But whether or not it was a carefully prepared plan, one thing could not have been premeditated: he could not have known that we would fall in love with each other.

The Dino episode was closed for ever, but on a note of love. The message he had sent me was a strange form of keepsake, but a keepsake nonetheless.

The war news was excellent. Germans and Italians were reeling back across the Western Desert pursued by the victorious Eighth Army and the Russians, also, were on the offensive.

Then came the news, to us the most exciting of all, that the Allies had landed in North Africa at our end of the Mediterranean. Victory was not only going to be soon. It was near, actually geographically near, in Algeria. Algeria was French, Victory was on our doorstep. We felt we could touch it. In a few days – weeks perhaps – but anyway soon, soon we would clutch and clasp it.

We were so happy, too happy to notice the grim and threatening storm clouds rolling relentlessly towards us. We only saw the sunshine.

On the day after the landings Le Petit came to see me.

'Look,' he said. 'The Germans and Italians are going to occupy the whole of France. Regardless of the Armistice conditions. The Italians will occupy the south coast as far as the River Var. The Germans will take over the rest of the country.'

I looked at him in horror.

'You have nothing to fear,' he said. 'Absolutely nothing. You know the drill – we've seen it with the Jews many a time. When the Italians want to arrest somebody they go to the Prefect and ask him to issue a warrant. He tells the police, the police tell us. You only know about people like Ailhaud and Cotoni. But we have many friends in the police, far more than you would imagine. Don't worry. Nothing can happen to you.'

'All the same, to be on the safe side I'd like to have an alternative identity, just in case.'

Le Petit shrugged his shoulders. 'All right, if you wish,' he said, humouring me. 'But it's quite unnecessary. What name do you want?'

'It's got to be the same initials. We've had them embroidered on the sheets. M.C. Let's say Monique Charpentier. And Mother can be Anastasie Charpentier.'

Le Petit brought me the sets of papers in the name of Charpentier and I hid them in a large bag of dried beans which we had in the kitchen.

'We're moving the office to Marseilles,' Le Petit told me. 'But we're leaving young Roman here as liaison. If you want us for anything ring him up – here's his number. Don't mention a place of meeting on the phone. But use 13, rue Grimaldi – the Italians don't know about that, we're pretty sure.'

'And you really think it's safe for me to stay in Nice?'

'Perfectly safe. And we may need you in a hurry. So this is the most convenient place for you to be.'

On 10 November he came to say good-bye. So did Colonel Jacobson. He was, he said, going somewhere near Carcassonne so that he would be near the Spanish border if he should have to flee suddenly. Simon Cotoni, too, was quietly leaving Nice.

On 11 November – the anniversary of the Armistice of 1918 – the Italians paraded down the Promenade des Anglais, the plumes of their helmets waving in the breeze.

I tried to keep cheerful but Taudu sensed that I was worried.

'Darling, don't worry. We can hire a car and go to some little village – anywhere you like. Your mother, you, Dougo and I. The Italians and the Germans can't have troops in every corner of France. We'll find somewhere where we won't be disturbed. Anyway, all these other people have gone.'

'I know. But I can't. Not without orders. I mean I've been specifically ordered to stay.'

But beneath the brave words I was frightened. I felt things were closing in on me. I no longer had the reassuring presence of my colleagues. I was on my own, exposed. A premonition of doom pressed upon me.

By the evening I was in a state of high nervous tension. Mummy and Taudu were listening to gramophone records but I, who love music deeply, could find no comfort in it. I slipped out of the room and took down a suitcase from the top of one of the cupboards which we had built. When Mummy came in to see what I was doing she found me feverishly sorting out pullovers and putting them in the case.

'What are you doing?' she asked.

'I don't know,' I replied. 'I really don't know. No, I'm not worried.'

And in a way I was not. I had implicit faith in Le Petit and the officers of our organization. And what Le Petit had said removed any possibility of sudden attack on me. I must trust their judgment. But I could not.

Taudu was already asleep when I came to bed. He was snoring. I lay awake, confused and bewildered. In my agony I tried to pray. But God was nebulous. I felt I was not getting through. I could not visualize God. But I could visualize my grandfather.

'*Help* me, Grandfather. *Help* me,' I pleaded. I spoke the words aloud and I could imagine the wise old face smiling down at me, the eyes alight with kindness and humour.

'Help me,' I repeated, but calmer now. 'Take care of me, like you always used to do.' I was using the tone which I had put on when I was a little girl trying to get him to give me another chocolate.

I was soothed, and able to think coherently. Every instinct told me, urged me, to flee. But I stubbornly refused to act on the warnings. I would go, but not until I had permission. I had been ordered to stay and I would obey these orders. Even at the cost of my life. To obey those orders had become an obsession. I knew it was madness to remain but I could not go. I was paralysed, frozen within my own destiny.

Now that I could think clearly I saw what I must do. I would not disobey the orders – no, no, never. But what I could do was to get the orders changed. As soon as I could I would telephone Roman, the young liaison officer, and arrange a meeting. Then I would make him telephone Le Petit and obtain permission for me to go. Anywhere, it did not matter. As long as it was out of the Italian Zone.

We had not been able to get a telephone installed in the flat, so I would have to use the one in the concierge's little hutch at the bottom of the stairs. I would have to wait until morning, when he would be up.

I lay, praying, hoping, despairing, praying again.

The black rectangle which was the window became grey, then suffused with the colours of the sunrise. Half past six. The concierge would be up by now.

I slid my feet into my bedroom slippers, flung my dressing gown round my shoulders and went down.

The concierge's wife was cleaning the stairs.

'I have to make an urgent phone call. May I?'

'Of course, mademoiselle.' She rose to her feet and opened the door of the little hutch. I waited until she had returned to her place on the staircase, out of earshot, then I lifted the old-fashioned receiver from its hook. The telephone was hung on the wall, rather high, and I had to stand on tiptoe to reach the dial.

I could hear the number ringing. Brr, brr. Brr, brr. At last a sleepy voice spoke. I recognized it as Roman's.

'Yes?'

'It's me. I want to see you. I must see you. Urgently. Immediately.'

'Right. What time?' Brisk and alert.

'Half past eight. No – quarter to nine.'

'*What?*' He was incredulous. 'You wake me up at this hour of the morning to make a date for two hours ahead. No, two and a quarter. You must be mad.' He slammed down the receiver.

I reached up and put mine carefully back on its hook. Roman was right. I must be crazy. To make an appointment two hours ahead when every minute counted was bad enough. But then, quite gratuitously to add another quarter of an hour was utter folly. Inexplicable madness.

I climbed slowly up to the fifth floor. Several times I stopped and nearly turned round. But if I did telephone Roman again and tell him I had to see him at once, that I could not wait two hours, he would be so furious that he probably would not come at all. I plodded on.

My mother was still asleep. So was Taudu. Only Dougo was awake, demanding to be taken out.

'Ah I can't be bothered. Use the table leg if you want to,' I told him. 'I couldn't care less.'

I was past caring about anything. Dazed, I wandered about

the flat like an automaton. Into the sitting room, out again, into the dining room, out again, on to the balcony. Then I sat in dumb misery, waiting for it to be time to go.

So long did I sit, stupefied, that in the end I had to dress in a hurry. The first stockings, the first skirt, the first pullover which came to hand. I opened a drawer and pulled out a headscarf.

'I'll come with you,' said Taudu. 'You'd better wear a coat – the mornings are getting chilly.'

'I'll only be about half an hour,' I told Mummy. 'I'm just going round to see Roman.'

'You're not going out like that, are you? Without any make-up on?'

'Haven't time.' I glanced at the marble clock, Mother's pride and joy. It was eight thirty-two.

I was far too overwrought to wait for the slow old lift so I started off down the stairs with Taudu a pace or two behind.

Down to the fourth floor. Half-way to the third I heard steps coming up. As I turned the corner I saw four men mounting the stairs.

Involuntarily I stopped. The leading one was so obviously Italian. Not only was his handsome face Italian but his clothes were smarter than a Frenchman's. Thinking that I had drawn aside to let him pass he muttered an apology. The emphasis of the consonants was undoubtedly Italian. The three men following him were more shabbily dressed but the fact that they were wearing soft hats instead of berets, as Frenchmen would, indicated that they too were Italian.

I felt sure that they had come for me. I went down to the landing and paused to listen. Were they going on past the fourth floor? Taudu pushed me. He, too, realized the danger.

Outside the house there was a car with a Rome registration. Taudu and I darted down the first street where we could not be seen from the windows of the flat. Then, certain that we were not being followed, we hastened on to 13, rue Grimaldi. It was only a few hundred yards.

'Go back,' I said to Taudu. 'And if the coast's clear come straight back and tell me. If you're not here in fifteen minutes I'll know that those men did come for me.'

I told him the number of the room and the secret knock – four quick taps, a pause, four more taps very close together. Taudu kissed me and started off down the street. I ran upstairs.

Roman was there before me, half asleep and angry.

I told him what had happened. He smiled patronizingly.

'It's all imagination,' he said. 'They may have been Italians – though I doubt it – but they weren't after you. That's for sure. You know as well as I do that they have to make any arrests through the French police.'

'I tell you they have come for me.'

He shook his head slowly. 'You've been under a tremendous strain. You're suffering from hallucinations. I don't blame you, mind you. Anybody would who's done what you've done.'

'Listen. Those men *were* Italian. They have come for me.'

The young man laughed.

'Nonsense.'

'If it's nonsense Taudu will be back any time now. He's been gone eight minutes already. If he isn't back in another seven we shall know.'

For seven minutes we sat in angry silence. Taudu did not come. Another ten minutes. Taudu did not come. Another. Another. No Taudu.

'Burn all the records,' I told Roman.

'Oh for God's sake!' he exclaimed, exasperated. 'You really are crazy.'

'Didn't you notice,' I said, 'that Taudu hasn't come back?'

Roman drew in his breath. 'Oh don't be ridiculous. Look, just to prove how absurd you're being I'll go round to your flat myself.'

'No! No, you mustn't.'

But it was no good. Roman had made up his mind.

'Very well,' I said. 'I can't stop you. But for God's sake be careful. Walk quietly up the stairs. Don't take the lift, it's noisy. When you get to the flat whatever you do don't ring the bell. There's a little trapdoor behind a grille. It's got a crack in it. You can't see much but you can get a peep through it.'

'All right, all right.'

'And – Roman this is important too. If they are in the flat don't come back here. You'll be followed. Go to Louis Bermond and send him to me. Don't try to come yourself.'

His arrogant laugh drove me mad. I knew that everything was lost.

'Roman, did you hear?'

But he was already out of the door and running down the passage.

I sat down to wait.

It was in this room, three years before, that I had experienced one of the highspots of my life. I recalled that day. The Admiral, courteous, complimentary. And me, cool and self-possessed, brushing it all away but secretly bubbling inside. Then it had been a palace, hung with chandeliers, the air heavy with the scent of orchids, a dream. Now it was a shabby prison, a nightmare.

Roman did not come. Bermond did not come. Taudu did not come. Nobody came.

Steps in the passage outside. No, going straight past. More steps. Hesitating outside. I clutched the side of the hard wooden chair. The steps went on again.

It was not surprising. It was a big building, offices and apartments. People coming and going. Leading their lives. But not me. I was suspended in time.

No food, no cigarettes. No cigarettes. No cigarettes.

Sooner or later the Italians would come. I must prepare myself. I must act with dignity. I hated to be caught like a mouse. I must not be pale in the face and my hands must not tremble.

'You have been condemned to death in Rome.' Marlene's words beat in my brain. At the time I had not taken them in, but now I had to face them squarely. With their inevitable consequence.

What would it be like to die? Quick, of course, an execution would be quick. No pain. But before – would I be brave and proud? Or would I crumble and collapse?

And in this way I spent all the morning and afternoon. Sometimes I think I must have slipped into unconsciousness. For now and again I was surprised to see how far the hands of my watch had travelled since I had last looked. And sometimes I shook it and held it to my ear, unable to believe it had not stopped. I was day-dreaming – but day-dreaming a nightmare.

When the evening came I could hear steps passing the door, going home. Home. What would Mummy feel when I was dead? And Taudu? Thank you, God, for Taudu. He will look after her.

Darkness. Stillness. Silence.

Four taps on the door. Pause. Four more.

I sat staring at the door, unable to move.

Again the knocks. I shuddered and heaved myself to my feet. I opened the door.

Louis Bermond stood there.

I had known Louis for some time. He was a sort of jack-of-all-trades in our organization. In his forties, one of those French artisans who has a natural talent for turning his hand to anything. Whatever job Louis was given he did efficiently without argument.

'We'll talk in the car,' he said, taking my arm. I stumbled down the stairs. Louis had to half carry me. It was dim in the street. The lights were not bright in Nice at that time, especially not in a sidestreet like the rue Grimaldi.

Louis told me that he was taking me to a house in the suburbs where his girl-friend and her sister lived. What had happened to Mummy and Taudu? He did not know. He only knew that when Roman had arrived at the flat he had peered through the crack in the peephole and had seen some men walking about. Evidently he had been too arrogant to take my advice and had marched up to the door regardless of the noise. Anyway, the Italians had heard him and one of them opened the door. He invited Roman to enter. Roman took one look and fled. He raced down the stairs out into the street where he jumped on to the tailboard of a passing lorry and was carried away. He had now gone to rejoin the rest of our organization in Marseilles. But one thing he had done for me – he had alerted Louis.

It took an age to reach the little house, bumping along in the slow old car.

'I've seen Ceccarelli,' Louis informed me.

'Who's he?'

'A detective, one of the top men in the police. He'll find out what's been happening at your flat.'

Thérèse, Louis's girl-friend, and her sister greeted me as if I were making a social call. Here I was, crawling in like the sole survivor of an earthquake, and they expected me to make polite conversation. And polite I had to be. I was a fugitive and they were sheltering me at enormous risk to themselves. I tried to make myself grateful.

Before Louis left he promised to return next day, as soon as he had news from this Ceccarelli. He would, though, have to choose his time. He was, he explained, a married man and his wife was already suspicious. He had to be careful, therefore, not to visit Thérèse too often or to stay too long.

It added to the nightmarish quality of this whole hideous situation that it had to be contained within the pattern of every-day existence. These matter-of-fact people must go on living their ordinary lives. The only thing which mattered to me in the entire world was to know what had become of Mummy and Taudu. To them it was of far greater importance that Madame Bermond should not find out that her husband was with his girl-friend.

I slept, exhausted. The next day was torture, torture such as I had never imagined. Far, far worse than the day before. What had happened to Mummy and Taudu? I could do nothing. I could not telephone anybody or leave the house. I had to wait for Louis to slip out when his wife was not looking. And all the time I had to say, 'thank you, how kind' to these two women, I had to behave myself in case they threw me out. I wanted to scream, to cry, to have hysterics. But I must smile and answer their trivial, banal questions.

At last, in the evening, Louis came.

He had seen Ceccarelli. Mummy and Taudu had been taken by the Italians. At first to a headquarters in Nice itself and now it was thought that they had been whisked over the border to Genoa. It was not a formal arrest. There had been no warrant, no permission from the Prefect. It was illegal. Kidnapping.

The handsome Italian I had seen mounting the stairs was Doctor Barenco, an evil and cruel official of the OVRA who had already made himself feared. He had told the concierge to telephone him immediately if I should return. If the concierge gave him information which would result in my being caught, Doctor Barenco would pay him a hundred and fifty thousand francs.

Ceccarelli had decided to fight Barenco with his own weapons.

If Barenco had gone outside the law, very well, so would Ceccarelli. His plan was this. He would take four armed men to the flat. He would get the concierge to telephone Doctor Barenco and inform him that I had returned. When Barenco came to apprehend me Ceccarelli would seize him and hold him hostage against the release of my mother and Taudu.

It was a gangster plot devised to beat a gangster.

Ceccarelli had gone to the flat. The concierge had telephoned Barenco. Ceccarelli and his armed men had waited.

But nobody came. Barenco must have suspected a trap.

Two days later Ceccarelli himself came to see me. He was young, my own age. He had an agile brain and the self-confidence inspired by a large private income. He was a detective because the work fascinated him, and for no other reason. He told me that many of the officers in the police were working underground, closely in touch with our own organization.

'But not the Commissaire, Nivello,' I said, remembering how hostile the man who arrested Zimdin had been to the Deuxième Bureau.

'Oh him. He isn't in Nice any more. He's gone to Vichy, where he belongs. We've got Pierre Sauvaire now, as Commissaire. He's a hundred per cent anti-Nazi.'

The news Ceccarelli brought was comforting. He now had definite information. Mother was in a prison in Genoa. But it was a prison run by nuns. I thought of those wonderful women who had treated me with great compassion in Lucerne. At the hands of women like that she would come to no harm. In any case when the Italians discovered that she really knew very little they would release her. Taudu, too, was in prison in Genoa. But as he did not know very much either he also would be released soon.

I was soothed and reassured. Even of Dougo there was good news. The concierge had him, feeding him with a spoon as we had done.

But the relief was only temporary. Ceccarelli, cheerful and confident, could not rouse me from my lethargy for long. I was still in a state of shock. Numb, not feeling anything any more. Not caring what went on round me, emotionally drained. I went through the routine of the day as if drugged. I nibbled at the food I was given without appetite, without tasting it. I forced myself to answer the sisters' endless silly questions. I was the victim of a disaster and I had nothing left. My senses were dead.

Ceccarelli made me recount to him every detail of that dreadful morning. And it was only when I went over the events with him that I realized how remarkable my escape had been. How it had hinged on so many tiny and unrelated chances.

If I had not suddenly changed the time of my meeting with Roman from half past eight to quarter to nine – and changed it absolutely without reason – I would have left the flat before the Italians reached the house. I would not have known they were there and when, thirty or forty minutes later, I had concluded my business with Roman I would have returned to the flat and found them waiting for me. I would have walked blithely into their trap.

If the ancient lift had been able to carry four people the Italians would have used it. I would have been on the stairs, going down while they were in the lift going up. Again, I would not have known of their arrival and would have returned after seeing Roman.

If I had dressed with my usual care and put my make-up on, Doctor Barenco would almost certainly have asked me who I was. But it cannot have occurred to him that I might be the elegant Marianne Chabot. Drab and insignificant as I was, he probably thought he was passing somebody's char.

Most remarkable of all the chances which had saved me was the precision of the timing. If I had left five seconds earlier I would have been far enough down the staircase for the concierge to see me from the hutch where Doctor Barenco had just enquired which floor I lived on. The concierge, in all innocence, would undoubtedly have pointed me out to him.

If I had left five seconds later Doctor Barenco would have met me higher up the staircase and would have realized that I could only have come from the fifth floor.

Going through it all with Ceccarelli I remembered that Mummy had queried my going out with no make-up and that I had glanced at the clock. Seeing that the time was eight thirty-two and knowing that it would take me ten or twelve minutes to walk to the rue Grimaldi and climb the stairs of number thirteen I realized that if I did not go at once I would be late for my appointment with Roman.

'Lucky the clock kept good time,' remarked Ceccarelli.

'Oh it always did. Mother found it in a junk shop. It was a great treasure – her favourite thing in the flat.'

'It undoubtedly saved your life.'

'Yes.'

Chapter 15

After I had been ten days in the little house with Thérèse and her sister, Ceccarelli completed his plans for my escape.

It was beautifully done. He had thought of everything. Nothing was left to chance. I, the second most wanted person in Nice, would be spirited away from under the noses of the OVRA.

That I was the second most wanted person in Nice was literally true. By this time Ceccarelli had had a sight of the list of suspects and condemned persons which OVRA had drawn up in order of priority. At the top of the list was Simon Cotoni. Next was Marianne Chabot.

Now policemen began to appear like archangels from heaven, to help me. Ceccarelli himself drove me to the station in a bullet proof police van, like an armoured Black Maria. Not to the main station at Nice but to the smaller one at Cagnes-sur-mer. Here he bundled me quickly into the train where a grey-haired man had kept a seat beside him in the corner. He was Pierre Sauvaire, the Commissaire de Police who was on his way to an important conference in Vichy. The Italians and the Germans – and indeed the French themselves – would hesitate to question a man of such authority whose high position made it obvious that he was one of the prominent French officials who conceived it his duty to work closely with the conquerors. I was safe beneath his wing.

This extremely able and tough policeman was gentle and kind. He stroked my hand comfortingly, and gave me a sandwich, and ersatz coffee from a Thermos flask.

A couple of years later it was my affidavit, together with those of others in the Underground movements whom Pierre Sauvaire had befriended, which saved him from the vengeance of the Free French on a charge of collaborating with the enemy.

We arrived at Avignon at three o'clock in the morning. Two plainclothes policemen were awaiting me on the platform. Monsieur Sauvaire continued his journey to Vichy and my escort took me to a house which they knew to be safe.

As we walked through the darkened and deserted streets I shivered with the cold. Winter had started early and it is always colder in Avignon than on the coast. The wind perpetually sweeps down the valley of the Rhône with the ice of the Alps in its breath.

The house was ancient, empty, and filthy. If it had not been for the war it would have been demolished years before. Long ago it had been deserted by its owners and since the war tramps had dossed down there, fugitives had hidden.

I sat dully on the dirty bed. It stank of urine.

In the morning one of the plainclothes men returned and took me to the police station where, so as not to arouse suspicion, I sat on a bench with the criminals until the Commissaire was ready for me.

Commissaire Autrive was a distinguished looking man in his late fifties. He asked me courteously how he could help. It would perhaps be better, he said, if I were to tell him the whole story from the beginning so that he would be able to judge what assistance I most needed.

I began my story in a confidential tone. But Monsieur Autrive was a little deaf. He kept asking me to speak more loudly until I was shouting my secrets nearly at the top of my voice. But when I had made him hear what I had to say Monsieur Autrive acted decisively. He promised to get in touch with Le Petit and sent one of his plainclothes detectives with me to a small hotel. The room was unheated but it was clean.

There was a basin with a tap – cold of course. So at least I could wash. But I had no fresh clothes to put on. When my stockings had become too impossible I had thrown them away. The clothes I had were barely adequate for Nice – for Avignon they were ridiculously thin. Even though I had worn them for eleven days I kept them on when I crawled under the eiderdown. The cold was so intense that even if I had been in full health and high spirits it would have been an ordeal. In my present state with my vitality at its lowest ebb the cold numbed my sense completely. I lay and shivered. Unable to think. Unable to feel anything except cold and fear. Fear and cold. Cold and fear.

I did not have the strength to try to survive. All I could muster the strength for was to try to stop going mad. To try to keep breathing.

Louis had given me cigarettes. Not many. I hoarded them. I smoked them slowly. I relit them. I postponed lighting another.

The cold and the fear. Fear of going out, fear of speaking to people. Fear of life. I was not a person any more. No will, no hope. No feelings except two. Cold and fear.

Even the news that Le Petit was coming to see me did not rouse me from my lethargy.

He came. For over three years I had known Le Petit. We had established an easy, happy relationship. Like brother and sister. Uncomplicated. Sincere.

And yet Le Petit's coming brought me no comfort. The worm of nervous depression was wriggling at my heart, my mind. I could not react any more. My battery was flat.

He gave me four thousand francs. All the organization could spare. He told me that Louis would come. He would go to the flat and fetch my case. He would put in it some shoes, some stockings – things I would need. Had I any money, any jewels, hidden in the flat? Yes, I told him. A few jewels. Several thousand francs. Not well hidden. Not well enough hidden to withstand a professional search. Just well enough hidden to fool a hasty burglar. Le Petit nodded. Louis would bring them. Oh, and the ration cards, identity papers. In the sack of beans. Nobody would have thought of looking through that.

'What are you going to do now?' Le Petit asked.

For more than three years Le Petit had told me what to do. Slowly, slowly, slowly I faced the fact that my espionage career was over.

I had embarked on it with such high hopes. Hopes which had been realized. I recalled my triumphs. In Sicily, the map of the defences. Oh, and the defences of the airport. Then the military zone on the way to Mondello. The number of planes in the new Italian Air Force establishment. And Genoa. Those battleships. The film in the train, hidden in the curtain. Hyères. Ah, Hyères.

Perhaps not a triumph of espionage. But a triumph, what a triumph. And Admiral di Giamberardino's recommendation to prove it.

Then Beirut. Information to the British. Household, Astor. And Barjot.

My career. And now – nothing. All over. Shivering in a little room. Shivering with cold. Shivering with fear.

Mummy in prison. Taudu in prison.

'Isn't there anyone you can go to, anyone anywhere?' Le Petit asked.

'Nobody. Nowhere.'

He was very patient. 'How about Erna Fiehl?'

'Erna? Oh no. She moved, you know. To Marseilles. I can't go and see her.'

'At least you could ring her up. You'd have the sound of a familiar voice.'

'I'll think about it,' I said grudgingly. For so long the Deuxième Bureau had given me orders, organized my life, that I resented the fact that there were no longer any orders for them to give.

'I expect you to tell me where to go,' I said accusingly.

'Just for the moment I'm telling you to go downstairs and ring up Erna. Oh do try, for heaven's sake.'

With an ill grace I went to the telephone. Erna's voice, warm, concerned, thankful to hear me.

'Where are you? Avignon? I'll come to see you. Tomorrow. Yes. Tomorrow.'

Le Petit was relieved. He was worried to find me sunk in such despair and he knew that he could not come often to see me himself.

'You can't stay in Avignon for long. It's stiff with Germans. You'll have to lie low until the Italians get tired of looking for you. You might try going to Alès or somewhere near there. It's quiet round there – no Germans. You'll be quite safe.'

His train left at one o'clock in the morning. We said goodbye in that cold little room.

'We may never meet again,' I said.

'That's always a risk in our profession. But don't take it all so tragically. I'm sure everything will be all right.'

He certainly did his best to make it so. He must have been travelling all night and yet he managed to organize things so that

Louis arrived in Avignon with my suitcase a little after eleven o'clock. Several of the pieces of jewellery were missing and all the money had gone. Louis told me that the flat had been ransacked.

The risk he had taken in going there at all was enormous but he made light of it. His fearlessness, his steadfastness put a little stiffening into me. He was kind, practical and matter-of-fact, as always. He did not dramatize anything. When Louis was with me I had the feeling that nothing had happened. I asked myself what I was worrying about.

He would, he promised, keep closely in touch with the concierge so that he would know immediately Mummy and Taudu returned. They, of course, would not know how to get in touch with me. The remains of the Deuxième Bureau had left Nice and Madame Gauthier had been arrested. Le Petit had given me an address in Marseilles to which to write but not to telephone. Accordingly, Louis told me, it had been arranged that I should telephone Thérèse, his girl-friend with whom I had stayed.

'But whatever you do don't telephone from Alès or anywhere near where you settle down. The OVRA and the Gestapo are working closely together and they'd love to know where to find Marianne Chabot.'

Louis made all this sound such an everyday thing, like planning to meet to go to the cinema together. ('Allow plenty of time to get there. The buses aren't all that frequent.')

'Bye now,' he said and disappeared with as little fuss as he had come.

In that time of terror I was immensely fortunate to have stalwart and level-headed champions like Louis and Le Petit. And in the afternoon another appeared.

Erna arrived.

'Where are you going?' she asked.

'Somewhere near Alès. Le Petit says it's safe. Oh Erna, I don't know what to do. I don't know how to set about it.'

I ran my hands through my hair.

'It's easy enough. We just get on a train and get out at Alès.'

'We?'

'Hansi, you and I. By the way, I'm a Czech woman – which I am – married to a Frenchman – which I'm not. So Hansi has become Jean.'

'But Erna! You're not coming too, are you?'

'Of course. Somebody's got to take you in hand.'

A long time later Erna told me that she had intended to leave Marseilles in any case. So possibly I provided her with a convenient escape route. But at the time I knew nothing of this. I only knew that Erna, reliable, lovable Erna had come to the rescue. I felt the first stirrings of life within myself again. I was still living in a nightmare, a dull sullen nightmare, but the shadows were not stretching quite so far from the dark corners of my mind.

'I'll go straight back and pack. Most of my stuff is in trunks anyway. Never been unpacked. Meet me on the station at eleven o'clock tomorrow morning and we'll take the first train to Alès.'

The walk to the station was an agony of anxiety. I was so alone, so naked. Every time I saw a German soldier I wanted to rush up to him and say, 'Arrest me, arrest me. I'm Marianne Chabot. Arrest me, shoot me. Get it over.'

Erna alighted from the train like a duchess paying a visit. Beautifully dressed, hair perfect, with a mountain of expensive luggage, she was wholly self-possessed. She scooped me up and took me with her in the train to Alès.

It was snowing when we got there. I suffered terribly from the cold. She had warm clothes in her trunks – they would be transported from the station soon. Directly we had found somewhere to stay she would organize that. But no stockings! She had not thought of that.

We tramped through the snow to a dingy hotel. Alès was a dingy town, a mining town. There were no Germans but if they should come Erna would be conspicuous. There would be questions. Besides, it seemed to be impossible to get our ration cards honoured. We must move on. God, how tired I was of moving on! From Vienna to Venice. From Venice to Monte Carlo. From Monte Carlo to Nice. From Nice to Lyon. From Lyon back to Nice. Only to flee again. To Avignon. From Avignon to Alès. Now from Alès – where? For four years I had been moving on. Every time I reached solid ground it gave way beneath me. Four long years.

This dreary town was impossible. Move on.

We took a train going in the direction of Nîmes. A slow train, crowded. We stood in the corridor. I was next to an old peasant, a rucksack on his back. Black market farmstuff, no doubt. I told him we were refugees. Where could we live? Where could we find somewhere we could hope to get food?

Langogne, he said. You know Langogne? No, I did not know Langogne. The only place. No *Boches* in Langogne. Food in Langogne.

It was a railway junction, two hours beyond Nîmes.

A tiny hotel. Simple, but clean. A lovely dinner.

Erna strode out through the snow and found us somewhere to live. We could not stay in the hotel more than a day or two without arousing suspicion.

There was a small modern house, *La Villa des Violettes,* which had been built by a retired postman, Pierre Clavel. He had scraped and saved all his life – he only ate one of his chickens when it died of old age – to build this villa with the intention of letting half of it.

We trotted through the snow to the outskirts of the little village. *Les Violettes* was built of stone and everything was duplicated. We had two bedrooms, a sitting room, a tiny dining room, a kitchen. The Clavels had the same, in the other half of the house. Bathroom? *Bathroom?* Who wants a bathroom, *mon Dieu!* Oh all right.

Erna took charge. Carpenters were called in to make cupboards, the furniture must be arranged so. I sat in a heap in a corner while she organized everything.

I wrote to the address in Marseilles.

But I could not wait. It would take several days for a letter to come back to me. I could not wait all that time for news of Mummy. Of Taudu.

I took a jolting train to Nîmes. From the station I telephoned Thérèse.

'Your friend is back. But not your relation. Your *near* relation,' she added hammering it home.

'Where is he?'

'He's gone home. His home. Later on he'll come to see you. When he's sure it's all right.'

So Taudu was back! I would see Taudu. Soon. How wise to go back to Paris. To make sure he was not followed before he came to Langogne. I could trust Taudu not to lead the OVRA and the Gestapo to me.

My step was light, my heart was light.

I boarded the train. Crowded, of course. As I shuffled along the corridor I caught the eye of a man sitting in the first-class carriage. I looked away but it was too late.

'Mademoiselle Zukermanova, Mademoiselle Zukermanova!'

It was Nivello, the police officer who had interrogated Monsieur Zimdin. What had I heard about him? Vichy. Yes, that was it. 'Gone to Vichy where he belongs.' That was what Ceccarelli had said.

He squeezed his way out of his compartment.

'Ah, Mademoiselle Zukermanova. How nice! What is it — three years since we met? And where are you living now?'

'Near Lyon.' It was the farthest place from Langogne that I could think of on the spur of the moment. Nivello was the last person I wanted to see. He would consider it his duty to betray me to the Germans. To him I would be a traitor – if he remembered that I belonged to the Deuxième Bureau. But three years was a long time. There was a good chance that he would not remember.

He was a policeman. He remembered.

'Last time we met you were in with a bad lot. Those decadent Deuxième Bureau people. Well, you're well out of that. They were disbanded, of course. Directly after the Armistice. Good job too. It's people like them who cause all the trouble we're having today. They can't see where the future of our country lies. If France is to rise again we must collaborate with our German neighbours.'

'Of course, Monsieur Nivello. Tell me, what happened to Zimdin? Did you catch him in the end?'

Nivello shook his head regretfully.

'Alas no. Nothing I could pin on him, you understand. He left France soon afterwards. Went to South America I believe.'

'Really? Ah, we're slowing down for Langogne. This is where I change for Lyon. Good-bye, Monsieur Nivello. So nice to see you again.'

'Good-bye, Mademoiselle Zukermanova. So nice to have seen *you*. Take care of yourself.'

Oh I will, Monsieur Nivello, I will. Good-bye, good-bye, Monsieur Nivello, good-bye. God!

Chapter 16

November 1942

Mummy committed suicide in the prison in Genoa on 19 November 1942.

My readers will forgive me if I do not enlarge on this. Beyond saying that she did it to protect me from anything she might disclose under torture. She gave her life to save mine as surely as if she had shielded me with her body on the field of battle.

She lies in Genoa cemetery. That cemetery in which she had said to me, three years before, 'It's a perfect place. So peaceful. So beautiful. This is where I'd like to be buried.'

My friends did not tell me. It was not until the war was over that I knew she would never come back to me. Perhaps they were right. Shattered and battered as I was in that winter of 1942 I do not think I could have survived the knowledge. And no one, not even Taudu, had the courage to tell me.

Chapter 17

December 1942-May 1944

Taudu did not in fact go to Paris. He came straight from Nice to Langogne. However, he was very conscious of the danger that the OVRA might have released him so that he could lead them to me. He therefore hired a car and left Nice at night, making sure that no lights were on the road behind him. Next day he hired another car and drove in a direction different from that of Langogne in case the driver of the first car should be interrogated. Then he took a train and after several changes he came to Langogne.

His arrest and imprisonment had shaken him badly and there was constraint between us. I think that, without realizing it, he held me responsible for his misfortunes. What should have been a blissful reunion was a rather strained encounter.

And so it continued for ten days. Then Roman suddenly arrived. How many letters had I written to the address in Marseilles? Only one, to tell them where I was. Why?

'Because,' answered Roman, 'we think that address is blown. If it is you're not safe here for a second.'

It was then that Taudu rose to the occasion. He became exactly as he used to be, decisive, clear-thinking. But kind, so very very kind.

We told the Clavels that we were going to spend Christmas with friends in Nîmes and then got on a train going the other way. We got off at the next station, La Bastide, further up in the mountains. At three thousand five hundred feet the cold was intense and we had only the thin clothes suitable for Nice. But Taudu was determined that we should enjoy Christmas and for three or four days we managed to forget the war and our troubles. In that remote country district there was no shortage of food and we dined sumptuously on Christmas Eve before going to Midnight Mass.

Two days later Roman telephoned Marseilles and discovered that the fears of the address having been blown were groundless. He thereupon returned to Marseilles and Taudu and I to Langogne.

This scare turned out to be a false alarm but in some curious way it cemented the love between Taudu and myself. From then on we regarded ourselves as husband and wife. His real wife had indicated that as soon as it became possible she wished to divorce him and remarry – and he intended to do the same. But it would have to wait until the end of the war. Under the German Occupation an action of this sort in the civil courts could not be contemplated.

Taudu had to be very circumspect in his visits to Langogne and we were constantly in fear that he might have been followed. Whenever a car drove up the road we stopped talking and sat, like dogs with their ears pricked, to see whether it was going to pass the villa.

In Paris it was possible to buy luxury foods on the black market – if you had enough money. Taudu did have enough money, and he would arrive at Langogne with a suitcase crammed with *pâté de foie gras*. Not only did he bring this rich food but also rope and string from his factory. This we were able to barter with the local farmers and shopkeepers so we were never short of food.

But Taudu could not come often, and never stayed long. For the rest of that long winter and into the summer of 1943 I remained at Langogne, living in the house of the Clavels. Once I went to Tence where Le Petit was living with his wife and a brand-new baby daughter. As I looked down at the cradle I prayed that she might grow up in a world happier than that into which she had been born.

Le Petit was still active in the fight against the Germans. But now his antennae were pointing in a different direction. We no longer met as agent and contact but simply as old friends. For me it was frustrating that I could not be employed. But I realized that any contact with my previous colleagues could, if the enemy ever caught me, result in the destruction of the whole organization. So all I could do was to remain quietly at Langogne.

The excitement and the adventure had finished. Only the danger remained.

I envied Erna. She at least was able to carve a life for herself out of the dullness of that little snowbound village. She engaged in the black market. Capable and efficient as she was, she made it into a regular business. With the shortage of petrol and transport to get it to the towns there was plenty of food available in the country. Erna would buy perishable foods, pack them into a suitcase and take a train to Marseilles where she would barter her goods for things unobtainable in the countryside round Langogne, such as olive oil. Her trips were, of course, illegal, and she therefore carried them out with the maximum effrontery. She would plonk herself down in a carriage reserved for German officers – a thing no Frenchwoman would dare to do. She would chatter away in German, explaining that she, a German, was married to a Frenchman and that she was taking food to her family starving in Marseilles. She made the Germans lug her cases for her and pass them through the checkpoint.

For myself, there was little I could do. Gradually I came to realize that old Clavel knew that I was 'wanted' and very cautiously we let one another know that our sympathies lay with the Allies. Clavel had a friend who was in touch with the Resistance and I was occasionally able to give him information which would be useful to the Maquis. This came about because from time to time Monsieur Sauvaire, the police official under whose wing I had travelled from Cagnes to Avignon, came to see me. He had a high position under the Vichy Government and he would talk of the reorganization of the Vichy police – and of the German police and Gestapo. He never told me to pass this information to any force hostile to Vichy but it was clear that that was what he intended me to do.

Monsieur Sauvaire was typical of many Frenchmen at that time. They carried on with their duties so that the administration of the country did not break down. Yet they also did everything in their power to undermine the German authority.

Others, like Taudu, traded with the Germans and grew rich in the process. Ostensibly they were collaborators. In fact if they had allowed their factories to operate at less than full capacity their employees would have been drafted to forced labour in Germany. And Taudu – and many like him – gave large sums of money to the Maquis and other organizations which went to make up the many forms of Resistance.

On a secret radio we listened to news broadcasts from Algiers and from London. Eagerly we garnered every scrap of information about the bombing, of the sea battles, of all the events taking place in the great world beyond the parish boundaries of our little village.

Then came the Allied landings in Sicily. I pictured the activity on that stretch of coastline which I had photographed. Those long guns in their yellow and green camouflage, silent for four years since then, would now be belching a weak defiance at the remorselessly advancing ships. The news became more and more exciting. Sicily over-run. Italy invaded.

At last the news which I had waited for above all else. Italy had capitulated. It was Giuseppe Castellano, my old acquaintance from Sicily, who, together with Marshal Badoglio, signed the Armistice document. Soon, soon now, my mother would be released. The agonizing months of separation, of acute anxiety would be over. Mummy would come back.

She did not. She could not. But I did not know.

Germany's reaction to the Italian surrender was swift and violent. Brushing the Italians aside, they took charge of the defences of the whole long peninsula. I realized with the deepest dismay that I could not expect that Mummy would be returned to me until the Germans had finally been driven from Italian soil.

The excitement which had flared up in me subsided. The wind catches the dying embers of a bonfire and a flurry of sparks flies upwards. Then the wind drops and the bonfire relapses into dullness.

But life at Langogne was not all sorrow. Mentally I could escape though physically I was trapped. There could still be fun, laughter. Games with the thirteen-year-old Hansi – whom we had to remember to call Jean. The life of that sturdy village community – it would have been wrong to remain aloof. And old Clavel. I formed a great respect for him. He knew perfectly well that, for the sake of his own skin and those of his wife and daughter, he should tip the wink to the Germans that he was suspicious of his lodger. Yet he risked them all being blown up with the house.

That dear old postman! I could not help teasing him. One day a mouse appeared in the dining room which we rented from him.

'I will get a trap at once,' he announced.

'No, no, Père Clavel. The mouse is my guest.'

He did not know whether I was joking. But he remembered that when he had bought some white rabbits as emergency rations I had made a pet of mine and refused to have it eaten. So he left the mouse alone.

Next time Taudu was expected I asked him to bring me a toy mouse. I put it in a dark corner of the hall. The hall was common to both halves of the house so I could not claim that I had the right to invite the mouse there. I could only protect a mouse in the sanctuary of the rooms I rented.

'Père Clavel, Père Clavel! A mouse!' I called.

The old man tiptoed towards the corner. Then he snatched off the blue beret which he always wore, indoors and out, and swept it down on to the mouse. Taudu and I watched his face. First the triumph of the hunter, then bewilderment and finally the realization of the truth.

'Ah, again! Once more I fall into your trap! But this is the last time. You won't catch me out again.' But I did. In those dark days it was silly little jokes that kept us going.

When a month had elapsed since Italy made peace with the Allies, Taudu and I decided that I might risk a visit to Paris. While the OVRA had undoubtedly passed my name to the Gestapo it seemed to us unlikely that, now that Italy had changed sides, the Germans would bother about anybody not on their own 'wanted' list.

But there remained one risk, a very real one, which was that I might be caught in one of the police swoops and carted off to forced labour in Germany. An able-bodied woman of just under thirty was fair game. Only mothers with young children were exempt. Again I resorted to false papers. This time they were issued by Clavel's friend, the link with the Maquis. French papers were more than an identity card – they listed the bearer's date of birth, place of birth, date of marriage, particulars of family, places of residence and other details. He provided a complete set in the name of Tardieu, which happened to be what the Langogne grocer was called. He also produced a photograph of a five-year-old boy whose particulars were included in my papers.

Thus equipped, I went to Paris. I always stayed in hotels – a different one each time. At that time Paris was surprisingly normal – at least on the surface. There were German uniforms everywhere, there were few cars and very little food. Otherwise, at first glance, Paris seemed a normal city. But one did not have to be there long to realize that there were many deep under-currents – and the deepest and strongest of them was fear. The Métro was still running. But, to save electricity, every other station was closed. It was always an anxiety to see whether the train would slow down before a closed station. If it did the probability was that it would be stopped there for a Gestapo check of the passengers. White-faced passengers – Jews, wanted people, men and women whose papers were not in order, or who were simply suitable for forced labour were taken away. The rest of us watched them go, powerless, terrified, deeply thankful that it was them and not us. Relief drove out compassion.

Then there was the nightmarish event of taking hostages. In the context of the attempted genocide of the whole Jewish race – and they only killed six million of them so the object was not achieved – the death of one innocent man is of no importance, unless you happened to know that man. He was a doctor, not a Jew. He was called out late one evening and he left his home in such a hurry that he forgot to take his papers. After he had attended his patient he called in at a police station to ask for a pass to protect him on his way home. It so happened that the superintendent in charge of the station knew him well and he stayed to drink a cup of ersatz coffee and to chat.

Suddenly the Gestapo burst in. The Resistance had committed some act of aggression and they were bent on revenge. They gathered a sample of the riff-raff which lines the benches of any police station late at night – drunks, tramps, petty thieves. Then they came into the superintendent's office and saw the doctor. They asked who he was.

'A doctor,' replied the superintendent. 'A friend of mine. He has been out late on a case and he . . .'

'Ah,' said the Gestapo officer. 'A doctor. An intellectual. Just what we want.'

They took him away and shot him.

It was during that winter that I had need of a doctor myself. Sharp pains in the chest. Everything was an effort. My head swam.

He diagnosed double pneumonia.

I ought, of course, to have gone to a hospital. But who could tell what incriminating things I might shout or mutter in delirium? It was a risk which could not be taken. Instead I had to be nursed by a courageous friend, Edith Levy. There were no medicines, no drugs. The only thing the doctor could recomment was oysters. Real oysters were unavailable – I had to make do with the Portuguese variety, small, deep shelled and tasting – to me – even more revolting than those I had swallowed to please Taudu in Cannes. Edith Levy brought me these oysters. Just to walk through the streets was dangerous for her, even though she hid the compulsory Star of David beneath the lapel of her coat.

Slowly I regained my health, very slowly. In those grim times there was little to encourage convalescence. A pall of fear hung over Paris and the shortages became so acute that just to exist was a tremendous effort of will. One cold day I was hurrying along when suddenly I noticed a smell of delicious hot food. I find smells immensely evocative, and this smell of steaming sauerkraut took me straight back to the Vienna of my youth. I saw that I was passing a canteen for German soldiers.

I went in. I was the only woman, except for the one on the desk and the waitress. Undoubtedly I was the only French customer. Nobody queried my right to be there. I suppose they assumed that I was secretary to some German official or something of that sort.

I used the canteen regularly after that, and the soldiers chatted freely. Obviously, they must have reasoned, I was perfectly safe or I would not have been there.

For some time I had been irked by the fact that I had no information to pass to Marseilles. Now, besides getting a square meal I was back at my old task of reporting troop movements.

'I was talking to a soldier with badges like yours last week,' I would say. 'He told me how terrible it is on the Russian front.'

'He was pulling your leg. Our unit's never been near the Russian front. We're in Normandy.'

It all went down in invisible ink and was posted to Marseilles. I was back in business.

Troop movements were important. We all knew that the Allied invasion could not be long delayed and every scrap of information about the forces lined up to oppose them was valuable.

At last the invasion came. After the agonizing uncertainty of the first few days we knew that in the end the Germans would be driven from France. We would only have to keep going a little longer.

But the German grip on Paris did not slacken. If anything the interrogations and the arrests intensified. 'It's almost an advantage to be a Jew,' Edith Levy remarked. 'There are so many new and exciting categories of wanted people now that the Boches hardly bother about Jews any more.'

Taudu had a friend called Martin and one afternoon when they were both away I promised to go and see Madame Martin. The door of the apartment was opened by a man in Gestapo uniform. I had no chance of running away. He took me to the officer in Madame Martin's drawing room. Beside the officer was a man in civilian clothes, the interpreter. I knew that I could expect no mercy from him. Nobody can be forced to be an interpreter and only the most dedicated pro-German Frenchmen volunteered for the job.

The officer took my bag and opened it. He handed the identity papers to the interpreter. My heart constricted as the officer himself drew out a letter which I always carried in my handbag. I kept it with me because it was a love letter. From Taudu. But it was more than that. It was a blueprint for our future – all the wonderful things we would do when France should be free again. Then there was a page of abuse of the Boches, clever, witty, just the mixture of mockery, hatred and contempt that maddened them. The word 'Boche' itself was enough to get us into bad trouble. (The Germans knew it was derogatory and forbade its use. Instead, because of the colour of their uniforms, we called them 'the green beans'.)

The officer held the letter up to the light to see whether there was anything written between the lines. Satisfied that there was not he handed it back to me. He did not read it.

'Ask her what she's trying to hide,' he told the interpreter.

'Nothing,' I replied when the question was translated.

'Then why are you so pale?'

'Because I'm frightened.'

'Ask her why she is frightened.'

'Who wouldn't be? To be interrogated by the Gestapo! It's terrifying.'

Evidently it was the right answer. When it was translated – and I noted that it was accurately translated – the officer grunted and turned away.

But my ordeal was not over. The interpreter beckoned me to follow him. He took me into Monsieur Martin's study and motioned me to the chair behind the desk. He himself sat on the corner of the desk and looked down at me, swinging his legs. His eyes were blue and cold. He opened my book of identity particulars and glanced at the first page.

'Ah, born in Langogne. I know Langogne. A charming village. But remote. A little self-contained village of peasants.'

He took a case from his pocket and offered me a cigarette. I stretched out my hand to take it and then drew back when I saw that it was the dark, bitter tobacco.

'No thank you. I don't smoke those.'

'You prefer English and American?'

He did not say 'English and American cigarettes'.

'I prefer *tabac blond*.'

He took hold of my hand and began to read from my papers. Every time he read out an item he ticked it off on my fingers.

'Born in Langogne. Married in Langogne. Had a child in Langogne. Lived all your life in Langogne. What – with hands like these? Nonsense.'

He flung my hand angrily aside.

'Look here,' he said with sudden passion. 'I don't know who you're working for and I don't care. But for God's sake get some better papers than these. Lived all your life in Langogne! Langogne indeed! Oh get out of here!'

Why he spared me I never knew. Many collaborators turned their coats when they saw the German defeat approaching but the interpreter did not do that. He was pro-German – of that I had no doubt. And those Frenchmen who were pro-German were more zealous than the Germans themselves, like religious converts. Perhaps he saw that the German domination of France was crumbling, the German Army disintegrating. They would not take him with them when they went. That he must have known. He was doomed. At the hands of his own countrymen he could expect no mercy. And yet, in a bitter savage way, he showed mercy to me.

Paris was a bewildering place in the last year of the war.

Chapter 18

February-October 1944

Towards the end of February 1944 Taudu and I decided that it would be safe to take a flat together. The Germans, we judged, had their hands too full to worry about one secret agent. They were being pressed in Russia and in Italy and it was inconceivable that they would bother to track me down.

Taudu found a palatial apartment which occupied the whole of one floor at 2, Chaussée de la Muette, a quiet road close to the Bois de Boulogne. It had fourteen rooms, most of them enormous, and exquisite Louis XV furniture and tapestry. But there was no fuel for the central heating and we had to huddle round a tiny stove in the middle of the magnificent *salon*. The owners, who had discreetly moved to their farm in the country, were thankful to have it occupied in those troubled times when empty property was very vulnerable. Consequently they asked a ridiculously low rent – three thousand francs a month, only three times the cost of a short journey in one of the bicycle-rickshaws which had begun to appear on the streets of Paris.

There was virtually no traffic and consequently sounds carried for long distances. Almost every morning about six o'clock we heard something utterly horrible. The executions in the Bois de Boulogne. Perhaps a German soldier had been found dead, and ten Frenchmen were shot in reprisal, or saboteurs had been caught, or criminals or black marketeers. Guilty and innocent alike, this macabre ritual was meticulously carried out day after day.

It gave me an added incentive, if any was needed, to haunt the canteen and report to Marseilles any troop movements I could discover. This was the time when the Germans were re-arranging their dispositions to meet the coming Anglo-American invasion. From Marseilles I received a flood of enquiries as to the whereabouts of specific units and I was deeply thankful to think that my efforts were helping to build up a picture of the German order of battle. The range and variety of the questions put to me from Marseilles indicated that my reports were being read by people who could put the information to good use.

But once the invasion had started – that glorious sixth of June – I received no more orders from Marseilles. Letters do not cross battlefields.

As the Allied armies raced towards Paris the civil administration of the capital collapsed. The Métro ceased to run, there was no gas, no electricity. Even the policemen went on strike. At last they were on our side. There was spasmodic fighting between units of the Resistance rising in insurrection and the rump of the German forces of Occupation. The citizens of Paris would gather in excited chattering groups and suddenly scatter before a burst of fire. It was dangerous to go out of doors but nobody dreamed of staying in.

On the day we heard that the Americans were already at the gates of the city Taudu and I walked to the Trocadero. We felt a desire to mingle with the crowds, to add to and to share our excitement with theirs.

The great open spaces at the top of the two flights of broad steps were thick with people, laughing, talking excitedly, waving their arms.

We who were on the pavement heard it first. The sound of an approaching car. Could it be the Allies already? Surely not. They would come with a rumble of tanks, not the thin little phut-phut of a tiny engine. It came into view, this small shabby open car. The only occupant was the driver, a German officer. The people near us glanced quickly round. Perhaps they were looking for something to throw at this lone, defenceless Boche as he drove past – a stone, a grenade.

But he did not drive past. He stopped the car opposite the foot of the steps and got out. He tugged his jacket down and squared his shoulders. Then he thrust his hands in his breeches' pockets and began slowly to mount the steps.

The crowd fell silent. I looked round in anxiety. There had been so much bloodshed. So much slaughter. And now one more killing was going to happen before my eyes. That he would be lynched I had no doubt. This great milling crowd of hundreds and this one man, the last representative of the hated oppressors. The beaten army had straggled out of Paris. Just this one officer left.

On he went, up the steps, his face expressionless. On and on. The people pressed back to let him through, they rippled out of his way like a flock of sheep being jammed into a pen.

On he went, higher and higher. Every step was a provocation, an invitation to violence. Perhaps he was deliberately tempting Fate, forcing his own destiny.

In utter silence he reached the very top. Then he swung round and looked at the city spread out before him. The bridges over the Seine, the Eiffel Tower, the superb and haunting view of Paris. He withdrew his right hand from his pocket. He raised his hand to the brim of his cap and made a gesture, half salute, half wave.

He walked down again, his steps ringing out in the breathless silence. No expression on the pallor of his face.

Nobody spoke. Nobody moved. No hand was raised against him.

Every sound seemed amplified in the stillness. The click of the car's door closing. The whirring of its starter. The irregular firing of its tired old engine, the hum which finally died away in the distance.

Everybody started talking at once.

The day of joy itself. That hot August day of delight. Paris was free.

I would not say that the four years of anxiety and horror were cancelled out by this one moment of Liberation. But at the time it seemed like it. We went about in a state of euphoria, thinking neither of the past nor the future, only of the present, the wonderful, lovely marvellous present.

Paris came to life. The administration started up again, every day something happened to show that for the capital of France the war was over. There was an urgency in the air, now we can get on with living.

Soon, I knew, I would hear from the Deuxième Bureau – or whatever it would be called now it could regain its official status. Perhaps there would be a new mission. If so, I was ready for it. I was ready for anything.

Only a few days after the Liberation I met Simon Cotoni in the street. Looking more like Napoleon than ever this little Corsican was now very highly placed in the police. And very, very busy.

All wars have their ugly aftermath. There is a sudden sharp reversal of values. What was patriotic becomes anti-social. What was courageous becomes criminal. What was self defence becomes vengeance. What was encouraged must be stamped out. No effort had been spared, no risk had been too great, to get arms to the secret warriors. Now they must be disarmed at all costs. Cotoni was engaged in the mammoth task of restoring law and order.

'I'm at 14, rue Las Cases,' he told me. 'Give me a few days and then ring me up and we'll get together.' He gave me his telephone number.

When I told him that I had seen Cotoni, Taudu remarked, 'And soon you'll see another old friend from Nice. Directly the trains are running properly I'll send a man down to collect Dougo.'

If only we could send for Mummy as easily as that, I thought. But I knew that there was no hope of seeing her until the war was over. But she would be safe in the care of the nuns.

About two weeks after the Liberation I was sitting in the flat waiting for Taudu to return from his office. The bell rang. The old housekeeper was at the other end of the flat so I opened the door myself. Three tough-looking men pushed past me into the hall. They had the armbands of the Resistance and they carried tommy guns.

'Come with us,' said the tallest of them.

'Why should I? Who are you?'

'You'll find out. Come on.' He took my arm and propelled me out of the flat. I was not frightened. It was obviously all a silly mistake. The old housekeeper, who had appeared by this time, was not frightened either. She knew who I was.

They bundled me into a car and drove me to a hotel. They were not impolite. I was a little irritated at being taken in this peremptory way. But they were Frenchmen, no harm could come to me.

They took me into a room where a table had been pulled out

and a chair set behind it to give the room the semblance of an office. The tall man sat down.

I said, 'Tell me who you are.'

'We are the Deuxième Bureau,' he replied.

I laughed. 'So am I.'

I expected him to enjoy the joke. But he did not.

'Our information is different,' he said shortly. 'Now, answer a few questions. You and your husband are collaborators. Tell me the names of your friends.'

'You've got this all wrong. If you ring up the police chief, Simon Cotoni, he'll vouch for me.' I told him the number. My years of espionage experience had taught me to carry such things in my head.

He took no notice. And that frightened me. If they had really been from the Deuxième Bureau or any official organization they would have telephoned Cotoni right away. I realized that they were not any official body at all. I looked round at the unshaven, unsmiling faces. I looked at the tommy guns and rifles. At the table with a blanket over it. This must be the twentieth-century edition of what a tribunal in the French Revolution looked like.

They took me to another hotel, a small one which they had obviously taken over completely. It was at 4, rue Léopold Robert, in Montparnasse. They took me upstairs and pushed me into a room. They were not rude but they were getting rougher.

In this room were several women, sleek well-dressed women. One was crying, one was shouting. None knew why they were there.

About midnight I was called and taken to a room by myself. I had not eaten since lunch. When I wanted to go to the lavatory I had to knock on the door and a boy with a tommy gun would unlock it and escort me along the passage. The room was on the second floor so there was no hope of escape.

In the morning I was taken down one flight of stairs and into another room set up as a tribunal. None of the men I had seen on the previous day was there. But behind the makeshift desk sat a handsome young man in the uniform of an Army lieutenant. His smart appearance was a welcome contrast to the scruffiness of my captors.

I was immensely relieved. The presence of an Army officer

indicated it was an official enquiry after all. There was another man, older, and a civilian. They conferred in quiet tones. I could not catch what they said but I realized that they were Corsicans.

Then the lieutenant started to interrogate me. I told him about my false papers, that my genuine ones had been blown up in Nomurat's safe in December 1942 when the French Fleet and the Naval installations at Toulon had been destroyed to prevent them from falling into German hands.

The lieutenant cut me short.

'I must tell you that our information is that you have been spying, not for the Resistance but for the Germans. Your position is very serious. I will do what I can for you but I must warn you that your position is very serious.'

'If you really want to help me telephone Simon Cotoni. He'll sort out this whole wretched business in a moment.'

'Yes, yes, of course,' he said politely.

I told him the telephone number. He made no attempt to write it down. It was clear that he had not the slightest intention of telephoning Cotoni.

I was taken back to my room. In the afternoon they brought me a bowl of very weak soup, scarcely more than warm water. But at least it passed for hot food.

In the evening a middle-aged Corsican came to my room. He offered me a cigarette and when he lighted it for me I could see his face. (It was dark and there was no electricity.) It was a kind face and I was not frightened of him.

'Why are they keeping me here, why don't they try to clear it all up?' I asked him.

'I really don't know,' he said. 'But don't worry, it'll be all right.'

He comforted me and gave me hope.

In the morning I discovered that my keys were missing from my bag. They had been there the night before so the Corsican must have taken them. Perhaps he intended to go to the flat and tell Taudu where to find me. Poor Taudu must be frantic by now.

Nothing happened. Nothing happened for nine days. Nine days of semi-starvation, of interrogation, of solitary confinement. I was not ill-treated in the sense that nobody hit me. But the mental anxiety was nearly unbearable.

In some ways it was worse than that terrible day in November

1942 when I had waited in 13, rue Grimaldi. For then I was hiding. Now I was trapped.

I knew that under the gaiety of liberated France ran deep undercurrents of revenge, of distrust, of violence. Retribution was swift and savage. Girls who had slept with Germans or even been friendly to them were having their heads shaved. How much more drastic would be the penalty for those who had spied for the Germans. I think if I had been one of those hostages facing execution by the Germans in the Bois de Boulogne I would have had more equanimity than in my present circumstances. It was a bitter thought that I had survived so much and, now that everyone else was free and life was beautiful, I should be in the gravest danger. And not from the enemy against whom I had fought so long. But from Frenchmen, the men of my adopted country.

I spent hours lying on the bed, too weak from lack of food to move much. It was an effort to get up and tap on the door.

The boy who opened it was one I had not seen before. He looked absurdly young with his blond hair and blue eyes. The tommy gun ought to have been a toy. Without speaking he held out a piece of bread to me.

I looked at him in astonishment.

'But why?' I asked. 'Why do you do this kind of thing to me?'

'I am a Catholic. We are all children of God. And however much we sin we deserve pity. I know you have done terrible things, wicked things, spying for the Germans.'

I was absolutely flabbergasted. I stared into those sincere blue eyes. Suddenly a shimmer of hope entered my soul. This boy might save me.

'Please come into this room, I must talk to you.'

He hesitated for a moment and then stepped across the threshold and closed the door behind him.

I asked him his age and his name. Eighteen. Bernard.

'Listen, Bernard. You're a Catholic and a good Christian. I'm sure you would always want to see that people act rightly. Justly.'

'Of course.'

'These people you're working for, they're not what you think. They're gangsters. Violent criminals.'

He began to protest.

'No, don't shoot me. You can prove for yourself that what I'm telling you is true. All you have to do is to go to 14, rue Las Cases. Ask for Simon Cotoni. Tell him Marianne Chabot is held prisoner here.'

He looked at me doubtfully. Then he turned on his heel and went out of the room. As I heard the key turn in the lock I felt weak. Probably I had uttered my own death warrant. If this boy went and told the lieutenant what I had said they would shoot me out of hand.

That night was particularly agonizing. Alone in the dark. Wondering. Fearing.

At nine o'clock in the morning I heard steps coming along the corridor. Loud purposeful steps.

Bernard flung open the door and the lieutenant stepped into the room. Behind him was a short man in civilian clothes.

'You're being transferred to the prison of Fresnes,' the lieutenant announced. The civilian caught my eye and I thought his eyelid flickered. But I did not dare to hope. Probably I had imagined it.

Downstairs he asked the lieutenant to give him a paper stating that he released me. The lieutenant, polite to the last, readily agreed. He wrote it out by hand and gave it to the civilian who put it in his pocket and thanked him. Then the civilian led me to a waiting car.

'Thank God that's over,' he said as we drove away. 'We're going to Monsieur Cotoni, of course.'

At rue Las Cases Simon Cotoni had an enormous office and a huge desk worthy of the Napoleon he so closely resembled. He made me sit in a very comfortable leather-covered armchair and tell him the whole story.

'Thank God that boy came to me. Of course we've been searching everywhere for you – the hospitals, the morgue, everywhere. In the end we came to the conclusion that you must have been kidnapped by the Germans.'

'No. By the French.'

'These are difficult times. Some of these people far exceed their duties. Will you do me a favour? Go home and see if anything is missing. Come straight back here and tell me.'

All I wanted to do was to go home to Taudu and stay there.

Preferably to sleep for a week. But I obeyed Cotoni.

'All my jewels have gone,' I told Cotoni when I returned. 'I didn't have much. Most were stolen in Nice. Taudu has replaced a few – oh and he gave me a gold twenty-dollar piece.'

'I thought they would have gone,' Cotoni commented. 'That's why they stole your keys.'

He leaned forward and pressed a buzzer on his desk.

'Bring him in.'

A policeman opened the door and brought in the handsome lieutenant from the rue Léopold Robert.

When he saw me sitting in the big leather-covered armchair smoking a cigarette he staggered. The blood drained from his face and I thought he would fall.

Cotoni addressed him in Corsican, reading from the list I had given him.

'I want these things back. I'll give you three hours to bring them. If you do I'll overlook everything else. I care very much for this woman. She has done fine things for France. She is a heroine. And she has suffered many losses. I do not want her to suffer any more. Least of all from a Corsican – a fellow countryman of my own.'

'But my God! How can I recover these things now? All the loot has been split up.'

'I do not even accuse you of having stolen these items,' Cotoni replied coldly. 'But they were certainly taken by men under your command. You are responsible. Have these things here within three hours.'

He nodded to the policeman and the lieutenant was led out.

He was back before the three hours were up. With him he had the little suède bag in which I kept my few pieces of jewellery. Cotoni tossed it to me.

'See they're all there.'

'Yes. Except one little bracelet. And instead of *one* twenty-dollar gold piece there are *twenty*.'

Cotoni frowned but his lips twitched.

'Another mistake. So many mistakes. But this one is on the right side. Keep the dollars. They'll make up for the bracelet.'

And that was the end of that.

I went home. I kissed Taudu. I kissed Dougo. I had a bath. I sank into my own bed.

I slept for twelve hours. Then I telephoned Simon Cotoni.

'I'm in a precarious position,' I told him. 'I feel in terrible danger here. Now that they know they made a mistake they might come and take their revenge. Double.'

'I'll be there at midday.'

When he came he gave our dear old concierge a gun. A gun!

'Let nobody in. Nobody you don't know. Nobody must enter this building unless you are absolutely sure of them. You must not hesitate to shoot.'

The old man gaped. Napoleon-Cotoni swept away.

The lieutenant was arrested on a charge not connected with me. Bernard, Bernard was a good boy. Taudu took his gun away and gave him a job with the *Corderie du Nord*.

Chapter 19

October 1944-April 1945

'You simply cannot go about with false papers any more,' Simon Cotoni told me firmly. 'I've saved you once, thank God, but next time I might not be able to. You *must* get hold of your real documents.'

I went to the *Ministère de la Marine*. After the casual intimate atmosphere of my meetings with officers of my own organization I found it all very formal and bureaucratic. I was shuffled and shunted until at last I found myself in front of an officer called Jonglez. He listened sympathetically and attentively.

'Do you mind coming back tomorrow? In the meantime I'll look up your file.'

'*File?* How can there be a file?' I thought of the Armistice, of the Occupation and the hasty flight of my organization's office to Marseilles, that terrible day in November 1942 when Mummy and Taudu had been arrested and I had been forced into hiding, of my clandestine meetings with Le Petit who had told me that, because I was 'blown' he dared not employ me any more, of the months at Langogne, the surreptitious visits to Paris, the reports on the Germans in the canteen. Of all the defeats and disasters which France had suffered. The world had turned upside down not once but many times. What bureaucratic nonsense was this? How could there possibly be a file? Jonglez smiled. 'The enemy only occupied France. They didn't occupy London. Or Algiers.'

He sent me to the appropriate department which had the noncommittal name of *Direction Général Etudes et Reserches*. It was located in the Bois de Boulogne, very close to the Chaussée de la Muette.

It was here that, for the first time, I realized how great was the scope and organization of the Resistance. In the years since the

Armistice I had had glimpses of the way the fight was being secretly carried on – Nomurat in Toulon behaving as though France were still officially at war, Le Petit conducting his under-cover activities in Tence, Ceccarelli rescuing me and passing me on to the police in Avignon. But now I was able to see something of the administration which had controlled and co-ordinated all our diverse efforts.

Now that France was free again those who had been working secretly were able to emerge from the shadows. The very tight rules of security were relaxed and we were allowed to know each other's names. Le Petit was Lieutenant Palisse, André Guieux was the name of the man whom I had nicknamed 'The Admiral'. It was no surprise to me to find that he really was an admiral – he could not have been anything else.

These old friends and many new ones from the Naval Head-quarters soon began to use our flat as a sort of club. With its four huge reception rooms it made an ideal place for them to meet and to have private discussions. Taudu and I were happy to be able to provide this hospitality and we were careful not to go into rooms which were being used for these meetings.

Of all the people who came to the flat the one whom I was most pleased to see was Barjot. It had always been a dream of mine that one day he and Taudu might meet. Each had out-standing intellectual qualities and, to my great relief, they immediately took to each other. In their very different ways they were highly successful and they both had a fervent patriotism.

General de Gaulle, too, had great respect for Barjot's judg-ment, and it gave me a feeling of pride that it was I who had been privileged to listen – and sometimes to put in a word – to Barjot when he was wrestling with his conscience. His decision to leave France and to join General de Gaulle had been the right one. He had given invaluable service to the cause and, in proof that his immense capacity was recognized, he had now been promoted from the junior *Capitaine de frégate,* which he had been when I first knew him, to Admiral.

One who was not riding the crest of the wave was Pierre Sauvaire. On his way to Vichy he had seen me safely to Avignon. But now it was what he had done when he arrived in Vichy that was in question. As head of the police he was a self-evident collaborator. But the truth was different. He had felt that a position of power under the Vichy régime would give him the opportunity to save Frenchmen from the Gestapo. There were many instances, and many people came forward to aver that they owed their lives to Pierre Sauvaire. I was happy to be able to be numbered among them.

Perhaps the most exciting news I received soon after the Liberation was from Le Petit. (Palisse his name might be – for me he would always be Le Petit.)

A new mission was being planned. It would involve sending me to Italy. This was thrilling news. It had irked me that while I was cowering at Langogne others were risking their lives in the cause to which I was dedicated. But, while Italy remained on the German side it was not safe for any agent on the OVRA's wanted list to be employed. The danger was that under torture the agent might reveal information damaging to the French organization.

But now Italy had changed sides and the situation was entirely different. It was unlikely that the Gestapo, with so much on their minds, would bother about continuing the search for enemy agents whose names had been given them by their former partners.

Once again I experienced the tingling feeling, excitement mixed with apprehension, hope with fear, which, over the years, I had come to know so well. But the mission was postponed. Le Petit did not tell me why – secrecy was too deeply ingrained in us for him to tell or for me to ask. But I guessed that the situation in Italy was changing too quickly for the mission, whatever it might be, to be effective. I resigned myself to waiting.

One day Jonglez came to tell me that I had been recommended for a high decoration. But there was a snag; General de Gaulle would not bestow a high French honour on a foreigner. Would I therefore, Jonglez asked, consider taking French nationality?

For as long as I could remember France had been my ideal. For the past six years I had lived in France, suffered with and for France, worked for France. I had had French papers. But they had been false ones. Now they would be real.

It was as if I had been walking up a long dark drive with the house at the end never getting nearer. Now the front door had been flung open and a welcoming shaft of light beckoned me in.

✳

The decoration was the *Croix de Guerre avec palme,* the highest class of the award.

In the spring of 1945 the war was in its final phase but it was not yet over. It was still necessary to maintain secrecy, not to draw attention to the undercover services. I could not, therefore, attend an official investiture, nor could the award be published in the *Journal Officiel.*

It was Le Petit who told me, in a rather awed voice, that Admiral Barjot himself would pin the decoration on my breast at a private ceremony.

In arranging the 'private ceremony' Taudu came into his own. It would be held in our apartment and he would see to all the arrangements. All I was required to do was to order a suitable evening dress. I chose black velvet, very simple and plain. It would form a background for the red and green of the ribbon of the order and the medal itself would show up like a jewel on a cushion.

The ceremony took place on 11 April 1945, under a month before the German surrender. Taudu had engaged a firm called Rosell to do the catering and they were magnificent. First they decorated the walls of the flat with flowers in the form of naval symbols – anchors, ships' wheels, funnels, anything to do with the Navy. Then they filled the flat with flowers, with the colours of the ribbon of the *Croix de Guerre* as the theme. Taudu ordered a huge basket containing orchids for me.

The guest list had been approved by the head of the department and we had twenty-four people, nearly all officers and their wives, to dinner. All very formal. Then, after dinner, many more guests arrived. The waiters were excellent and they kept the supper buffet constantly replenished all through the night.

Admiral Barjot pinned the decoration on my breast and made a short speech. He ended on a personal note.

'What I myself owe to her, only Marianne and I know.'

I noticed several people look up quickly. But nobody asked what he meant.

Taudu had engaged a quartet and after the presentation we danced. It was a wonderful evening. My only sorrow was that Mummy could not be there. But I comforted myself with the thought that soon the war would be over and she would be released. Still nobody had told me.

I gazed round the room, imprinting every detail on my memory so that I could tell her about it. The handsome men in their blue and gold uniforms, the beautiful women in dresses made as only Paris can make them. The chandeliers, the banks of flowers, the waiters gliding about carrying silver trays, the head waiter and the *sommelier* in consultation beside the buffet. France, that great agricultural country produced food and to spare and now that the distribution networks were operating again there were no shortages – we could enjoy the sumptuous food in the knowledge that we were not depriving anyone.

Barjot and his wife stayed until two o'clock. With their departure some of the junior officers felt less constrained. The air had become heavy with the smell of rich food and tobacco smoke. Taudu opened a few windows.

Attracted by the noise, some policemen came in from the street to see what it was all about. Willing hands brought them glasses of champagne. More champagne. By this time the party was in full swing. We were young, we were happy, we were healthy. We were having fun.

Somebody suggested a *farandole*. So dancing and singing we wound our way, crossing and criss-crossing, through the big rooms. The policemen waved their batons, they blew their whistles, they directed the traffic.

It was seven o'clock in the morning before the last guest left. The party had lasted for nearly twelve hours.

Taudu and I stood by an open window. At this early hour nobody was stirring in the Chaussée de la Muette. But the traffic was rumbling in the thoroughfares of Paris. The city had come to life again. There were no more shots in the Bois de Boulogne.

Taudu pressed my hand.

'Happy?'

'Happier than I have ever been.'

He nodded, satisfied.

'And now,' I said, 'let's get some sleep.'

'Yes. But before we do I've got something to tell you. I saw my solicitor today – yesterday now. He says divorce proceedings have started. So, God willing, we shall be able to marry soon.'

Six months later Croco Taudu was killed in a car crash.

Historical Note

The Second World War was preceded by the Nazi occupation of Austria in March 1938, and of the Sudetenland in October. In March 1939 Hitler invaded the rest of Czechoslovakia. On 1 September his troops marched into Poland without any declaration of war. Ultimatums from Great Britain and France demanding the immediate withdrawal of the forces were ignored and on 3 September 1939 these countries declared war on Germany.

The autumn of 1939 was the period of the 'Phoney War'. Italy, Germany's partner in the Rome-Berlin Axis, unexpectedly delayed entering the war until the German successes early the following summer. By June 1940 the Nazis had conquered Norway, Denmark, Holland and Belgium; British troops withdrew from the Continent at Dunkirk and Marshal Pétain headed a French Government which sued for peace.

In London, General de Gaulle formed a Provisional National Committee 'to defend that part of the French Empire which has not yet been conquered by Germany and to free that part of France still under the yoke of the invader'.

The Pétain Government set up its headquarters at Vichy. The Germans occupied Northern France including Paris. Italian troops occupied Menton. The Vichy Government broke off diplomatic relations with Great Britain, its former ally.

For the next year the war was fought in the Egyptian and Libyan deserts and in the Italian colonies of North-East Africa. Except for the Axis occupation of the Balkans and the subsequent engagements in Greece and Crete there were no land battles in Europe, but intense naval and aerial activity.

In June 1941 Hitler attacked Russia. In December 1941 the Japanese attacked Pearl Harbour and the United States entered the war on the Allied side.

For the first part of 1942 the Axis partners – now joined by

Japan – were victorious in all theatres of war except that British Imperial and Free French troops occupied Syria and the Lebanon to forestall a pincer movement on the Suez Canal. By the early summer Italian desert forces and the German Afrika Korps were within a few miles of Alexandria and Cairo.

In the autumn of 1942 the situation changed in favour of the Allies. The British 8th Army's success at El Alamein and their pursuit of the Axis forces westwards across the desert, coupled with the landings of British and American forces on the coast of North Africa farther to the west, resulted in the expulsion of all Axis forces from Africa. The Germans reacted by moving into Unoccupied France, with the Italians occupying a short strip of the south coast. Early in 1943 the Russians began to advance, inflicting heavy losses on the troops which had been besieging Leningrad and Stalingrad.

The Allies landed in Sicily and then in Southern Italy. Mussolini was arrested in July 1943 and three days later the Fascist Party was dissolved. Italy surrendered to, and then joined, the Allies but the German troops fought on in Italy until almost the end of the war in Europe.

In June 1944 the Allies landed in Normandy and a further landing took place on the Mediterranean coast in August. In the same month Paris was liberated. The Allies liberated Belgium and most of Holland and at Christmas 1944, the Germans made their last great attack of the war, in the Ardennes. After initial successes they were driven back and the Allies mounted the final assault on German soil. On 28 April 1945 Mussolini, who had been rescued by Nazi paratroops but subsequently returned to Italy, was shot by Italian partisans and strung up to a lamp-post in Milan. Hitler killed himself in his bunker in Berlin on 30 April. By the first days of May nearly the whole of Germany had been overrun by the Allies and the war in Europe came to an end with the German surrender on 8 May 1945.

Japan fought on until August 1945.

In 1939 the average foreign exchange rate of the pound sterling was

France:	
Italy:	
United States:	
franc	176.10
lire	85.22
dollar	4.485

D E C I S I O N   No 406

On the proposal of the Minister for the Navy

General   de   GAULLE

President of the Provisional Government of the
French Republic, Head of the Armed Forces,

A. P P O I N T S

TO THE "ORDRE DE L'ARMEE DE MER"

— Mrs ZUKERMANOVA Edita, alias Marianne CHABOT

"She accomplished without a break, during
four years, several very fruitful missions on Foreign and
enemy territory.   She displayed, in the course of these
missions, wonderful qualities of courage, coolness and
intelligence, as well as technical ability.   Having lost
her parents on account of the enemy, escaped by miracle
from "L'OVRA" and the GESTAPO.   Having lost all her possessi
gravely affected in her health by these ordeals, she was
finally hidden and saved by the resistance.   This agent
always volunteers to serve".

This citation carries the award of the CROIX
de GUERRE with palm.

This decision will not be published in the
"Journal Officiel" of the French Republic.

PARIS, 16th February, 1945

Signed: de GAULLE

I the undersigned, P. COLLEU,
Consul Attache to the French
Embassy, hereby certify this
to be a true translation of
decision No 406 dated 16th
February, 1945.

PARIS 2nd MARCH 1945

MINISTERE DE LA MARINE
ETAT MAJOR GENERAL
3ème Bureau

No 175 E.M.G.3/REC.

N O T I F I C A T I O N

SUBJECT: Appointment to the "Ordre de l'Armée de Mer" of
Mrs ZUKERMANOVA Edita alias Marianne CHABOT.

ENCLOSURE: Copy of the award No 406

I hereby notify you of the award No 406,
dated 16th February, 1946, appointing Mrs ZUKERMANOVA Edita
to the "Ordre de l'Armée de Mer".

Signed: Vice-Admiral LEMONNIER

I the undersigned, P. COLLEU,
Consul Attaché to the French
Embassy, hereby certify this
to be a true translation of
notification No 175 E.M.G.3/REC.
dated 2 March, 1945

STUDIES DEPARTMENT
   NAVY

C E R T I F I C A T E

     I the undersigned, Georges DEBAT, Lieutenant-Commander, Head of the Navy Studies Department, hereby certify that:

> Mrs ZUKERMANOVA Edith
> daughter of ZUKERMAN Hugo
> and PERNITZOVA Ana
> born in Vienna (Austria) on the
> 10th August, 1913

worked for our services from 1938 until the liberation in conditions which have motivated a proposal that she be cited to the "Ordre de l'Armée de Mer", currently underway, sent by the Director General of the D.G.E.R. to the Minister for the Navy.

          PARIS, 13th January, 1945

          (Signed) DEBAT, Lieutenant-Commander

I the undersigned, P. COLLEU
Consul Attaché to the French
Embassy, hereby certify this
to be a true translation of
Certificate dated 13th January,
1945.

MINISTERE DE LA JUSTICE

13, Place Vendôme, Paris (1er)

—=—=—=—=—=—=—=—=—=—=—=—

DIRECTION DES AFFAIRES
CIVILES ET DU SCEAU
————————

SCEAU   DE   FRANCE

No 33.842X44

FRENCH REPUBLIC

The Provisional Government of the
French Republic on the report of the
Minister of Justice

DECREES:

ARTICLE I

ZUKERMANOVA (Edith, Anne, Marie), born on the
10th August, 1913 in Vienna (Austria), living
in Paris,

is naturalized French (art.6, paragraph I, of
the law dated 10th August, 1927).

The Minister of Justice will implement this
decision which will be published in the
"Journal Officiel".

PARIS, 25th August, 1945

Signed: Mr. Jules JEANNENET and
Mr. Pierre-Henri TEITGEN

the undersigned, P. COLLEU,
Consul Attache to the French
Embassy, hereby certify this
to be a true translation of
the document, reference 33.842X44,
dated 25th August, 1945.

C E R T I F I C A T E

membership to the F.F.C.

References   No 107 693

Mrs ZUKERMANOVA Edith born on the 10th August, 1913 has signed a recruitement contract in application of decree No 366 of the 25 July, 1942.

Network: "S.R. MARINE"

The services as agent P I are carried out from the 13 November 1942 to the 30 September 1944 in the capacity of "chargé de mission" 3rd class.

Rank assimilated to Sub-Lieutenant by the National Endorsements Commission (for the duration of the mission).

PARIS, 8th August, 1968

Signed: CALLEC.

I the undersigned, P. COLLEU Consul Attache to the French Embassy, hereby certify this to be a true translation of certificate, references No 107 693, dated 8th August, 1968.

FRENCH REPUBLIC

MINISTRY   OF   STATE
IN CHARGE OF NATIONAL DEFENCE

DEPARTMENT OF ARMY PERSONNEL

Department:"Résistance"

No 107.693

C E R T I F I C A T E

of

MEMBERSHIP OF THE FRENCH FIGHTING FORCES

The Minister of State in charge of National
Defence, certifies that:

Mrs ZUKERMANOVA Edith
born on 10th August, 1913, in Vienna (Austria)
appears on the registers of the network "S.R. NAVY"
(Sub-Network PERRIER)

for the period 1st March 1941 to 12th November 1942
as permanent agent (P.1.)
in the capacity of   X   of mission   X   class
decision of   X   repatriated on   X
Rank assimilated for the duration of the mission
X   X

PARIS, 2nd July, 1971

Signed: CALLEC.

This certificate cancels
and replaces the one issued
on 6th April,1970 under the
same number.

I the undersigned, P. COLLEU,
Consul Attache to the French
Embassy, hereby certify this
to be a true translation of
certificate No.107.693, dated
2nd July, 1971.

C:O.L.

NAVY SECTION
211/309/MA-TB

15 MAY 1945

N O T E

for the attention of the HEAD OF THE FINANCE DEPARTMENT

SUBJECT   — Request for backpay for an agent

ENCLOSURE   — Report of Lieutenant PALISSE
Head of S.R.O./1 North Sector

      The enclosed report is being forwarded with my recommendation that it be acted upon for the following reasons:

      Madame ZUKERMANOVA is not an ordinary network agent, but a person of high calibre who proved herself even before the war in the S.R. Navy, where she took on difficult technical assignments, including one with Admiral BARJOT, Deputy Chief of Staff of National Defence.

      As a result of a mention in Naval dispatches, this high ranking Officer made a point of personally awarding to her the CROIX DE GUERRE in the presence of the Officers under whose direct orders she had served.

      Without going into details regarding the outstanding further services she rendered in Lieutenant PALISSE's network after the Armistice and until she went into hiding, may I add that this network was integrated into the D.G.E.R. with all its personnel and assets. It therefore seems only fair that its liabilities be also integrated, since the D.G.E.R. is alone in a position to settle this matter now that the Ministry for the Navy no longer has an S.R. budget.

Pour traduction
certifiée sincère
Londres, le 23-12-74

Le Consul Adjoint,

P. P. COLLEU,

Signed: G. DEBAT,
Lieutenant Commander,
Head of the Navy Section.

<u>TRANSLATION</u>

Pour traduction
certifiée sincère
Londres, le 23.12.7

Le Consul Adjoint,

P. COLLEU,

LIEUTENANT PALISSE
HEAD OF THE S R 0/1-NORTH SECTOR

LIEUTENANT-COMMANDER
COMMANDER OF THE NAVY SECTION

      I beg to inform you that Mrs ZUCKERMANOVA, a member of the Navy Headquarters Intelligence Service since 1938, has been paid until November, 1942, From that date, this person, recruited for the sum of Frs. 3.000 per month, has not received any further pay.

      At that time, I ordered her to lie low for several reasons.

1) - Her considerable activity in Italy for three years had brought her to the attention of "OVRA". It should be mentioned that her services are recognised by a Naval citation and the award of the CROIX DE GUERRE with palm.

2) - On the 11 November 1942 her mother was taken hostage by the "OVRA" at Nice.

3)   On account of this arrest, her health was severely affected.

4) - She was obliged to hide under a false identity and I considered that her incorporation in my network would endanger the security of the whole team due to the constant enemy efforts to trace her.

      May I add that this person has always been willing to serve and that I had to order her formally to remain in hiding.

      She has lost everything she possessed. Her flat was ransacked by the Italians when her mother was arrested.

      Finally, I intend to use her services on the forthcoming missions to be undertaken on your instructions in Italy, where she knows a great number of persons in key positions and can be very useful to us.

      I would ask you to approach the Finance Department so that Mrs ZUCKERMANOVA, who has never ceased to belong to our services and will return to active duties in the near future, may receive her back pay amounting to Frs. 90.000.

      May I draw your attention to the fact that the rate of Frs. 3.000, fixed in 1938, has remained unchanged until 1942.

                LIEUTENANT PALISSE
                HEAD OF THE S R 0/1-NORTH SECTION.

La Signorina Marianna CHABOT, governante dell'Hotel
Chateaubriand, dove è alloggiata questa Delegazione Nava-
le, si è prodigata perché ogni servizio risultasse di pie-
no gradimento di tutti, superando con la sua abilità e
previdenza le difficili condizioni dell'approvvigionamento.
Con la sua ottima conoscenza della lingua italiana e tede-
sca , col suo zelo e con la sua cura intelligente è stata
di grande utilità per questa Delegazione e per le altre Ita-
liane e Germaniche che sono state di passaggio nell'albergo.

L' AMMIRAGLIO DI DIVISIONE
Presidente della Delegazione
(Oscar di GIAMBERARDINO)

(Author's translation)

Italian Commission of Armistice with France

Naval Delegation

24th September 1940

Mademoiselle Marianne CHABOT, supervisor of the Hotel Châteaubriand where this Naval Delegation has been quartered, has given outstanding service to the delegation. She has ability and foresight, and has overcome all difficulties in provisioning the delegation. Her faultless knowledge of the Italian and German languages, together with her diligence and intelligence, enabled her to be of great assistance, not only to the members of this delegation but to all Italians and Germans passing through this hotel.

(signed)
        Admiral of Division,
        President of the Delegation,

                Oscar di Giamberardino.